Symbolism in Hindu Architecture

L. Peter Kollar

Symbolism in Hindu Architecture

As Revealed in the Shri Minakshi Sundareswar

Photographs by
Alan Croker

Aryan Books International
New Delhi

SYMBOLISM IN HINDU ARCHITECTURE

ISBN: 978-81-7305-204-0

First Published: 2001

Reprinted: **2023**

Published by:
Aryan Books International
Pooja Apartments, 4B, Ansari Road, New Delhi-110 002 (India)
Tel.: 23287589, 23255799; Fax: 91-11-23270385
E-mail: aryanbooks@gmail.com
www.aryanbooks.com

Printed in India

Books That Live!

Aryan Books International was established in 1992. Though it began as a commercial venture, business was only a part of the whole. The primary aim was to bridge the gap between the history taught and the real history of our country, and also to present its lesser known and sometimes deliberately neglected facets. In academia, the legacy of our art, culture and ethos was being undermined to perpetuate a narrative which left us looking weak, soft and lagging behind the so-called progressive West.

It was this narrative that we sought to contest. The journey over the last thirty years has not been an easy one. However, it gives us a sense of satisfaction to have possibly made a small difference by publishing over 750 titles written by the most acclaimed authors in the field. We have specialized in publishing ingenious and outstanding scholarship, both established as also fresh. While we focus on our long forgotten history, we also bring to the fore certain extremely important aspects of Indian art, culture and traditions.

Apart from pioneering content, we also ensure that our production quality remains the best in the business, as we continue with the mission to publish books that **Live Forever**!

We are also aware that this is just the beginning of a long journey. A long road lies ahead. A lot more needs to be said. A lot more needs to be explored. We assure you that we're on it with renewed commitment!

CONTENTS

LIST OF ILLUSTRATIONS

FIGURES

PLATES

INTRODUCTION

Hindu traditional symbolism (*Pratika*), whether verbal, musical, dramatic, iconographic, or – what is our main concern here – architectural, always refers to domains that are unknowable and inexpressible by sensation, emotion or reason.[1] This is the *raison d'être* of symbolism in traditional civilizations, where the main preoccupations are directed towards the understanding, the knowledge and the attainment of certain states which are 'superhuman': symbolism is used to communicate, as far as this is possible, the nature of the states in question. On the other hand, in civilizations where the tradition is no longer effective or has become largely unrecognizable, symbolism is lost, or what is worse, is subverted, since the chief preoccupation of the people shifts to the strictly human, even to the simply material or 'subhuman' level; traditional symbolism hence becomes 'superfluous' since all that is 'worth' communicating can be communicated in human terms. Symbolism thus not only escapes the attention and the understanding of such communities, but is also gradually despised by them, leaving the door open for certain anti-traditional influences to take hold of the symbolic language and to use it in a subverted sense.[2]

Of the several traditions still operating in a more or less recognizable way in the world today the Hindu tradition has preserved its continuity for by far the longest period and is still effective in a truly remarkable manner. Owing to its unbroken tradition, its reliable scriptures and written records of great antiquity and its rich symbolism developed in all fields of art, it is an eminently suitable field of study to acquaint oneself with a way of communication which is no longer effective in the West.[3]

All that belongs to the 'superhuman' order, or more precisely to the domain of metaphysic to which traditional symbolism refers, is unconditioned by space and time. A study in this field, therefore, cannot be validly undertaken from a logical or systemati, from a spatial or geographical, or even from a temporal or historical point of view. The systematic exposition or the tracking of the origin, development or style of certain symbolic forms or of symbolism as a whole will lie outside of our object and interest; no matter how helpful or fascinating the results of studies undertaken from such contingent aspects may be, they are irrelevant from the metaphysical, that is the symbolical, point of view. In fact, it seems that most of the enormous amount of research carried out by western scholars into the various aspects of Oriental traditions in the last hundred years or so – laudable and valuable as it is in certain respects – suffers from the failure to realize at the outset that the meaning of metaphysical doctrines will inevitably escape a materialistic mentality applied from the outside. 'It would be hardly an exaggeration to say that a faithful account of Hinduism might well be given in the form of a categorical denial of most of the statements that have been made about it, alike by European scholars and by Indians trained in our modern sceptical and evolutionary modes of thought'.[4]

This warning alone seemed sufficent to avoid an attempt to impose the 'physico-logical' mentality peculiar to the modern West upon a study of Hindu symbolism which belongs essentially to the order of metaphysical. A study of this kind will remain true to the spirit of the tradition only if it is approached from the *inside* and not from the *outside*. This means that one has to acquaint oneself with the doctrinal concepts of the Hindu tradition, understand its terminology and develop any such study with the use of the same terminology; not to be deliberately obscure, but, on the contrary, to express precisely the concepts that reveal themselves in the architectural symbolism of the Hindus, concepts for which precise equivalents are difficult to find in the West.[5] However, if there are no precise equivalents, there are certain analogical correspondences which will be elucidated not so much with specific reference to western doctrines – such an attempt may well form part of another study – but rather with the use of the symbolism inherent in words and expressions that are of western origin and carry concepts peculiar to the West. Above all, a study of this kind should be conducted with a concern not so much with the formulation of concepts as with the inherent truths that these concepts symbolize. These truths belong to an order that is, properly speaking, formless and therefore cannot be affected by the formal differences in the language, or in the conceptual thinking of the East and the West, nor even by their various forms of art.

Once the metaphysical nature of Hindu symbolism is understood, it will be viewed as transcending its particular form and its particular application. Adopting such a point of view it can be said that all Hindu symbolism refers to Brahma,[6] 'the unqualified and absolutely unconditioned Supreme Principle'[7] in one of its indefinite number of aspects. The choice of aspect, its form and application, is then not of paramount importance since the number of each of these limiting conditions can be taken as indefinite. The *point of departure* is then, so to speak, contingent or peripheral when compared to the *point of reference* which is truly essential. On the circumference of a circle no position can be more unique than another; it is the orientation towards the centre, which is adopted from any of these arbitrary positions, that becomes, because of its radial direction, unique. In short, this unique orientation is the essence of traditional symbolism, or, to use another terminology, it is its orientation corresponding to the radial direction and therefore connected with the 'Centre', which distinguishes sacred art from profane art.

This central orientation is also the structure of the present study. All considerations of the vast, teeming richness of Hindu symbolism are referred directly to the symbol *par excellence* which is the Shri Minakshi Sundareswar temple at Madura,[8] occupying the central position of this study. The structure of the study follows similarly the radial direction referred to, a pattern which also coincides with the physical path one would take by entering the temple from the outside, progressing within, reaching its core and, eventually, understanding it in its totality.

The Shri Minakshi Sundareswar is dedicated to Shiva and to his consort Parvati. It is a temple in the Shaivaite tradition which is not a sect, as many would believe, but an aspect of the integral Hindu orthodoxy. The Hindus, contrary to all appearances, do not worship several gods, but approach Brahma, the 'One without a second',[9] the 'absolutely unconditioned Supreme Principle' behind all distinctions, above all determinations, void of all attributions, the Principle of Being *and* Non-Being. If conceived as the unchanging Reality behind the universe, the macrocosm, it is denoted by the term Brahma; if conceived as the uncreated and uncreatable Spirit in man, the microcosm, it is referred to as *Atma*. In both cases the Supreme Principle is unqualified (*Nirguna*) and beyond any limitation, 'universal manifestation in its entirety being strictly nil beside Its Infinity'.[10] The first and highest of all determinations of the Supreme Principle is *Ishwara*, the 'Divine Personality', the Principle of universal manifestation unmanifest itself, nevertheless already qualified (*Saguna*). *Ishwara* enters into manifestation by His divine energy, will or power (*Maya*) and gives rise to the Hindu Trimurti, namely Brahma (now with accent, the masculine form), creative principle, Vishnu, the maintaining principle and Shiva, the transforming principle. Each of these principles has its own divine energy or power, *Shakti*, which is considered feminine or substantial in relation to its masculine or essential Being.[11] The *Shaktis* are then represented as consorts – Saraswati being Brahma's, Lakshmi being Vishnu's, Parvati being Shiva's.

The more exalted a principle is, the harder it seems for the human being to approach it, to worship it and to attain it. Consequently, the Hindus worship *Ishwara* as their personal God either in the form of Vishnu or Shiva or the Devi, very little attention being paid to Brahma. Those who worship Vishnu are the Vaishnavites and for them Vishnu is the symbol of the creating, maintaining and transforming principle. Those who worship Shiva are the *Shaivites* and for them Shiva is the symbol of the creating, maintaining and transforming principle. Those who worship the Devi, 'the Goddess', are the *Shaktas* (from the word *Shakti*), approaching *Ishwra* by way of His 'feminine' aspect of divine power or energy. Since we are concerned with the *Shaivite* tradition here, the symbolism related specifically to Brahma, Vishnu or the Devi will be outside our immediate interest.

Shiva and Parvati have two productions, or sons: Ganesha, the principle of approach, obstacles and wisdom and *Murugan*, the principle of fighting and justice. All these Divine Personalities have a great number – theoretically an indefinite number – of aspects and these aspects are known under different names and represented in iconographic symbolism by different forms. Minakshi, the fish-eyed goddess, is an aspect of Parvati and Sundareswar is an aspect of Shiva. It was under this form that he married a local maiden and this occasion is perpetuated in The Great Temple at Madura. The Shri Minakshi Sundareswar Temple is thus in its very name (*Nama*) the symbol of the union of *Purusha* (Essence) and *Prakriti* (Substance), unmanifested in themselves, but from which union and from which union alone universal manifestation proceeds.[12]

The authority of Hindu orthodoxy is the *Veda*, the sacred scriptures, transmitted orally for untold number of years and committed to writing for many thousand. 'The Hindus regard it as eternal, without beginning, without human authorship'[13] and 'it is the fruit of direct inspiration so that it is in its own right that it holds its authority'.[14] The *Veda* is the *Shruti*, which means a text of first authority, whereas other traditional writings are *Smriti*, a text which "derives its authority from an authority other than itself",[15] that is from the *Shruti*.

The *Veda* is arranged in four books, namely the *Rig-Veda*, the *Yajur-Veda*, the *Sama-Veda* and the *Atharva-Veda*. Each falls into two sections: *Mantra* and *Brahmana*. Usually the *Brahmana* section is concluded with an *Upanishad*. The *Upanishads* contain the purest metaphysical teachings of the Hindu doctrine. This section is also called the *Vedanta*, the 'end of the *Veda*'.

The teachings of the *Upanishads* were co-ordinated in a collection of extremely concise aphorisms known as the *Brahmasutras*, which together with other *Sutras*, *Shastras*, *Agamas*, *Tantras* and *Puranas*, belong to the group of texts known as *Smriti*.

The references of this study are based upon the *Vedas* in the first place and then upon the *Smriti*. Special attention is paid to the *Shilpa-Shastras* which deal with the arts in general, to the *Vastu-Shastras* which deal with the science of architecture and to the *Puranas* which are a collection of extremely beautiful myths of profound symbolic significance.

However, because of the necessary limitations of this study it has not been possible to refer to the Sanskrit texts in all instances, especially not in those which deal with the application of the doctrine from a western point of view. In all such cases the works of René Guénon, Ananda K. Coomaraswamy, Stella Kramrisch, Titus Burckhardt and Frithjof Schuon are being taken as authoritative since these writers were always most careful to remain truthful to the spirit of the Hindu tradition as it is interpreted in the West. Their works formed, in a sense, the basis for the present study; without this foundation the author's endeavour would have remained fruitless, misconceived and ill-channelled.

The author desires to acknowledge his debt also to Mr. Adrian Snodgrass for introducing him to sources of the Hindu tradition on his journey to India and Ceylon; to Professor J.M. Freeland who kindly supervised his work and offered valuable guidance and welcome suggestions at all its stages; and to Mrs. M. Conning who typed graciously and with painstaking precision the text.

Sydney **L. Peter Kollar**

NOTES AND REFERENCES

1. Cf. A.K. Coomaraswamy, *The Transformation of Nature in Art* (Dover, New York, 1956), p. 126.

   'In distinguishing thus a language of symbols from a language of signs I have in mind the distinction of symbol and sign drawn by Jung. A symbolic expression is one that is held to be the best possible formula by which allusion may be made to a relatively unknown 'thing' which referent, however, is nevertheless recognized or postulated as 'existing'. The use of any symbol, such as the figure '*Vajra*' or the word 'Brahman', implies a conviction and generally a conventional agreement resting on authority, that the relatively unknown, or it may be unknowable, referent cannot be any more clearly represented. A sign, on the other hand, is an analogous or abbreviated expression for a definitely known thing; every man knows, or can be informed, by indication of an object, as to what the sign means. Thus wings are symbols when they 'mean' angelic independence of local motion, but signs, when they designate an aviator'.
2. The subversion of symbols is not to be confused with the inverse analogies inherent in symbolic expressions. Moreover, most symbols can be taken in a beneficent and in a maleficent sense. All this is perfectly legitimate as long as the beneficent aspect is not confused with the maleficent aspect or as long as the maleficent meaning is not interpreted as beneficent. Precisely this is in what the subversion of symbols consists, which can even be furthered by using traditional symbols to convey quite distorted meanings they were never intended to carry. Such subversions may operate without the understanding, nay, even with the best intentions of certain individuals, which, incidentally does not in the least diminish their adverse effect. Cf. René Guénon, *The Reign of Quantity* (Luzac, 1953), pp. 241-248.
3. One must forgo here any further explanation regarding the nature of the Hindu tradition, its mode of operation and its relation to what remains of the western tradition. These questions have been fully dealt with by René Guénon in his 'East and West' (Luzac, 1941).
4. A.K. Coomaraswamy, *Hinduism and Buddhism* (Philosophical Library, New York), p. 3.
5. The present study develops the meaning of Hindu symbolism exclusively *ab intra* and makes no attempt to elaborate correspondences – which are extensive indeed – with other traditions of the Far East or of the West.
6. René Guénon, *Introduction to the Study of the Hindu Doctrines* (Luzac, 1945), p. 225. Cf. p. 227: 'In order to avoid all confusion it should be observed that the word Brahma, without an accent, is neuter, while the word Brahma with the accent, is masculine; the use, current among Orientalists, of the single form Brahman, which is common to both genders, has the serious disadvantage of obscuring this distinction'.
7. René Guénon, *Man and His Becoming according to the Vedanta* (Luzac & Co., 1945), p. 25.
8. The Great Temple at Madura, South India, is a typical example of a great number of South Indian temples built in the last period of Hindu architecture (approx. A.D. 1500-1800). Its style is classified according to the Shilpa-Shastras as Dravida and was built by the Nayaka dynasty of Madura. The sanctuary is said to be started by Viswanath, the first king of the dynasty, in 1520 and completed by Tirumala (1623-59). It covers an area 852 ft. x 729 ft. and is said to contain some 3,00,00,000 sculptures.

The deity is in worship even at present and at the time of the author's visit (1960) all signs indicated the presence of a fully alive tradition.

9. Swami Nikhilananda, *The Upanishads* (Phoenix House Ltd., London, 1957), Vol. I, p. 34.
10. René Guénon, *Man and His Becoming*, *op.cit.*, p. 25.
11. The terms 'Substance' and 'Essence' are used throughout this study according to the concepts elucidated in Greek and Scholastic philosophy.
12. This is clearly not the place to give an account of the Hindu doctrine and the foregoing remarks should in no wise be taken as such, not even as a simplified form or as a skeleton, since such attempts would have no other purpose than to denature and to distort its integrality. All that was intended here was a nomenclature of principles (personified as gods) which will be constantly used and referred to in the following and which, for the sake of those who are new to the subject, has been presented in a chain of causal derivation.
13. Swami Nikhilananda, *op.cit.*, p. 1.
14. René Guénon, *Man and His Becoming*, *op.cit.*, p. 19.
15. Shankaracharya quoted according to René Guénon, *ibid.*

PART I

THE GATE AND ITS GUARDIANS

This Self (*Atma*) is represented by the syllable *OM*, which is represented in turn by letters (*Matras*); the conditions are the Matras and the Matras are the conditions: these are A, U and M.

Vaishwanara, whose seat is the waking state, is A, the first *Matra*, because it is the connection and also because it is the beginning. He who knows this verily obtains all his desires and he becomes the first.

Mandukya Upanishad
Shruti 8.9

1. GANESHA, GOD OF BEGINNING

According to the *Shiva Purana*, the birth of Ganesha (Pl. 1) is related as follows :

The origin of Vighneshvara is different in different aeons of creation. I am relating to you now the story of the birth of this god as it took place in the *Shveta Kalpa.*[1] Once upon a time, *Jaya* and *Vijaya*, the two companions of Parvati, suggested to her that though she had Nandi, Bhringi and others among Shiva's attendants as her servants, still it would be better for her if she had a person as her own servant. Parvati took the advice in good part and it so happened subsequently that, on one occasion when she was bathing in one of her inner compartments of her mansion, Shiva not knowing where she then was, went into the place where she was bathing. Parvati realised the value of the advice of her friends fully then and resolved upon creating a person who would be a faithful servant to her. She took a little of the dirt on her skin and created out of it a lovely being and ordered him to keep strict guard at her gate so as not to allow anyone inside without her permission. Once, Shiva himself happened to go to meet his consort, but could not get access into her apartments, as the new gatekeeper would not allow him in. Shiva then tried entreaties and threats, none of which proved effective. He then resolved upon forcing his way in somehow. On noticing this, the new *Dvarapalaka*[2] administered to Shiva a few cuts with a cane and drove him out. Incensed at the behaviour of this insignificant servant of his consort, he ordered his *Bhuta-Ganas* – host of demons – to kill him at once. In the fight that ensued Shiva's host of demons were completely defeated and driven away. Then Vishnu, Subramanya and others tried, on behalf of Shiva, their strength with Vighneshvara and met with no better result. Then Parvati, on seeing that her son Vighneshvara was fighting single-handed against powerful opponents, sent two minor goddesses to his help. They drew towards themselves by their mysterious power all the missiles aimed against Vighneshvara and protected him from injury. Finding thus that no direct methods of attack succeeded against Vighneshvara, Vishnu thought of using strategy and with the aid of his *Maya*, he caused confusion. Thereupon the two minor goddesses, finding their presence no longer of use there, returned to Parvati. It then became easy for Shiva to cut off and remove the head of Vighneshvara.

The news of the destruction of her son was conveyed to Parvati by the sage Narada; and on hearing it she became so angry that she created a thousand fighting goddesses to bring trouble on all those who took part in the destruction of her Vighneshvara. These goddesses attacked the gods and made them feel very miserable.

To rescue the gods from this pitiable condition, Narada and other sages prayed to Parvati, who promised to restore peace as soon as her son was brought back to life. Shiva on hearing this, ordered the gods to proceed to the north at once and bring the head of the first living being they met and fix it on the neck of the beheaded son of Parvati. The gods immediately proceeded and came across an elephant; they cut off its head and brought it and attached it as directed to the trunk of Vighneshvara. That elephant had only one tusk and Gajanana (the elephant-faced Vighneshvara) has therefore, only one tusk even today and is known by the name of *Ekadanta*. When Parvati saw her son brought back to life in this manner, she felt pleased and took him to the presence of Shiva. Vighneshvara apologised to Shiva and the other gods for his past remissions in conduct and bowed in deep reverence to his divine father. Shiva was thereby highly gratified and conferred upon Vighneshvara the commandership over his own demon-hosts and anointed him as Ganapati. It is thus that Vighneshvara became Gajanana and *Ekadanta* and Ganapati.[3]

The *Skanda-Purana* gives a somewhat different account of Ganesha's birth by relating that Parvati created him alone by gently rubbing her body and thus producing 'a wondrous being with four arms and the head of an elephant.'[4] Parvati then commanded the Elephant-headed as follows:

> Oppose obstacles to men visiting Somanatha[5] and entice them to give up such a purpose by allurement of wives, children, possessions and wealth. But from those who propitiate thee by the following hymn do thou remove all difficulties and enable them to obtain the favour of Shiva by worshipping at his shrine of Somanatha: *Om*, I praise thee, O lord of difficulties! The beloved spouse of Siddhi and Buddhi, Ganapati, invincible and the giver of victory, the opposer of obstacles to the success of men who do not worship thee, I praise thee, O Ganesha! The dreadful son of Uma, but firm and easily propitiated! O Vinayaka, I praise thee! O elephant-faced who didst formerly protect the gods and accomplish their wishes, I praise thee! – Thus, continued Parvati, shalt thou be praised and worshipped on the fourth of each half month; and whoever previously invokes the god Vinayaka, no difficulties shall impede the attainments of his proposed object and a most beneficial result shall he derive from sacrifices, pilgrimages and all other devotional acts.[6]

These Puranic stories contain a wealth of symbolism about the 'nature' of the principle or 'spiritual function' which the embodied and personified form of Ganesha represents. As Vighneshvara, he is created miraculously by Parvati alone and is first intended as a 'servant' formed from 'a little of the dirt on her skin'. At this stage this 'wondrous being' is a production, or differentiation, of the Universal Substantiality for which Principle the supreme aspect of Parvati in this connection stands.[7] He is commanded to 'keep strict guard at her gate' and whilst he puts up his valiant primordial fight 'single-handed against powerful opponents' is as yet unmanifested Substantiality considered under the already limited aspect of its 'protective', 'withdrawing' or 'self-pressuring' tendency against the 'intrusion' of Universal Essentiality. That Vighneshvara is a principle beyond manifestation is clearly shown by the words that his 'origin is different in different aeons of creation'. It thus stands above, that is, it is primordial to the various cycles of manifestation in which it manifests differently. To be manifested, the victory of Essence is necessary over the protective tendency of Substance; this necessitates the 'act of sacrifice' by undergoing mutilation only to be resurrected in the manifested state, not any more as 'servant' but veritably, as 'son', because it is now the manifested result of the interaction of both Essence and Substance. The victorious Essence (Shiva) has a double function here: on the one hand He is 'incensed' and therefore mutilates, on the other hand He is 'highly gratified' and therefore 'anoints'. These terms seem contradictory only as long as the 'passage' from the Unmanifested into the manifested state is not recognized. Because of the inverse analogy[8] that exists between these states, the 'incensed' attitude in the Unmanifested corresponds to the 'highly gratified' one in the manifested, the act of mutilation to the act of anointment. It is thus that Shiva thence becomes the 'Divine Father' of the being, which entered in the manifested state and hence is known by the name of Ganapati.

By his elephant-headed body, however, Ganapati re-affirms his ontological link with Parvati, that is *Prakriti*, Universal Substantiality, for which Principle the symbol *par excellence* is 'the waters'[9]; the natural habits of the elephant are eminently explicit of its connection with this element.[10] Hindu symbolism draws, beyond the seemingly inexhaustible variation of anthropomorphic forms, also upon images derived from the animal and vegetable states and is no less careful and precise to symbolize with the inherent nature of the selected animal state, by analogical transposition, the 'inherent nature' of the principial state in question.

Ganesha thus assumes in his manifested state the same 'function' that was 'his' in the Unmanifestd, namely the protective tendency, or, if another ex-pression may be used, the 'reluctancy' of the undetermined Possibility to become determined and manifested. Whereas in the Unmanifested, this aspect of *Prakriti* was perceivable only in relation to *Purusha*, in the manifested state Ganapati becomes the 'guardian' of the *Purusha-Prakriti* pair in relation to man, by becoming the 'opposer' as well as the 'remover of obstacles' of 'men's desire' to transgress the bonds of manifestation (*Samsara*). He is therefore, revered by countless Hindus as the god of the obstacles and this function is clearly represented in iconography in more than one way. From this point of view the 'elephant-nature' of Ganesha reminds us of the relentless power of the elephant to overcome the seemingly insurmountable obstacles of the jungle, obstacles which cannot be negotiated by man without the aid of the beast. But obstacles may also be of a different kind: impractical to overcome forcibly but convenient to evade by slipping through. Ganesha's vehicle,[11] the rat, signifies this tendency in a frappant, even grotesque, but *a fortiori* in an eminently clear manner.

Ganesha holds two no less significant objects, the goad in his right, the lassoo in his left hand. As a remover of obstacles, he urges on his worshippers with the goad, only to hold them back with his lassoo, as the opposer of obstacles. His dual function is really only one: it is resolved, as eventually all duality is resolved beyond the 'appearances' of manifestation in his single person 'dreadful....but easily propitiated'. He is therefore worshipped at the beginning of every 'spiritual act', of every sacrifice, no matter to which 'more exalted' god is the sacrifice intended for. Without propitiating Ganesha nothing can succeed. He is the 'gatekeeper' of spirituality, the 'beginning' of every act directed towards spirituality, the 'point of contact' between the profane and the sacred, by whom and through whom alone is 'entry' into the higher states of the being possible.

The unequivocal differentiation between the profane and the sacred is also the central idea of every Hindu temple;[12] it is constructed upon sacred ground to 'build in' or to 'localise' the 'Divine Presence' as manifested in the world. It is primarily the 'sacred abode of the gods' and its use for human worship is, so to speak, a contingent aspect.[13] The temple's material form thus asserts, by its very existence, the difference between the sacred ground and the surrounding profane world. The link between these two separated realms is the 'point of contact' through which every 'passage' must lead and the Shri Minakshi Sundareswar temple at Madura establishes this in an even more formidable way than the personified and iconographic symbol of Ganesha does.

To understand the symbolic analogy just referred to, it is necessary to consider at some length the awe-inspiring nature and overwhelming intensity of architectural symbolism which stems from architecture's unique relationship with man. A full discussion of all possible aspects of this relationship would lead us too far from the central theme; yet, it will be advantageous to digress shortly and to elucidate certain conditions which affect architectural symbolism whilst they do not apply to other forms of art, more particularly not to other forms of representative[14] art.

In the first place architectural form is rigorously governed by the laws governing the material from which it is constructed and formed. This statement, strictly speaking, is true about sculpture and painting or other forms of representative art, but it could easily be shown that the degree of dependence upon these conditions in the latter group is far less significant than it is in the case of architecture. The difference, moreover, is not so much quantitative but rather qualitative. Sculpture's and painting's dependence upon the laws which govern their physical constituents is a problem real enough, but a problem that can be described as peripheral compared to the field of architecture where this problem becomes verily central. The connection between architecture and gross or corporeal manifestation is rigorously firm which is not the case in other forms of art. This condition limits architecture to a greater degree, but the very same limit applies to the human being in its corporeal modality and it is thus that architecture 'meets' man, being affected by the same limiting conditions.

Yet architecture embraces the human being even more firmly from another point of view. Since it is, by definition, a form of art which human beings can physically *enter* and in which and around which they can *move about* freely, architectural form will necessarily follow the conditions which govern the natural functioning of the human body, conditions that other forms of art can mostly ignore.[15] This condition limits architecture to an even greater extent, but this very limitation, being common to both architecture and man in principle, establishes an exceedingly strong bond between them that no other forms of art can hope to possess.

Further, since human beings can bodily *enter* into architectural form, this is the only form of art which establishes in the physical, or gross, state the manifestation of the exceedingly important concepts of 'outside' and 'inside', of 'the external' and 'the internal', or – to use the equivalent architectural terms – of 'mass' and 'space'. These concepts have very far – reaching symbolic interpretation in general as well as in the particular connection with the human being. Here again architecture alone is qualified[16] to extend symbolically this dual appearance to the principal order from where all manifested application of the principle of 'outside' and 'inside' derives.

Now, the accumulative effect of the foregoing relationships, on the one hand, can be expressed simply thus: architecture 'takes hold' of man whereas other forms of art have to be 'taken hold of' by him. In other words architecture establishes a link, a 'point of contact' with the human being firmly already in the lowest, that is, in the corporeal state and using this *punctum saliens* it develops symbolic communication into progressively higher domains even if the human being is in a passive mental state; other forms of representative art, however, must 'wait passively' – if such an expression is permitted – for the opportune moment when the human being is in the appropriate *mental* state, when he exerts his selective will in an active mode, to 'notice' the significant symbolic content which is to be communicated. In this latter case the human being will remain in most instances 'the onlooker', whereas in the former he becomes 'the experience'.

On the other hand the accumulative effect of the strong bond that exists between architectural form and gross manifestation in general almost forces a situation in which architectural symbolism has to correspond in every respect to the 'facts of life', that is to the conditions determining gross manifestation. In other words, whenever an architectural form is intended to symbolize principles of the higher orders, it has to correspond strictly to the manifested forms of the same principles in the gross order; or inversely, an architectural object of use can symbolize only the same principle from which its gross form is derived.

These rigorous conditions do not leave much scope in architecture for 'fantasy' or 'imagination' in the choice of symbolic expression; architecture therefore appears to be more limited in its operation than other forms of representative art are in theirs.[17] Not that symbolism in these latter forms of art would ever be based on wild fantasy or empty imagination, not in any case as long as it remains true to the spirit of the tradition; but in the case of architecture the more serious deviations or subversions are, as it were, prevented due to the 'central' nature of the necessary correspondences elucidated before. Moreover, these limitations placed upon the manner in which architectural symbolism operates are far from limiting the effectiveness of communication in any respect; on the contrary, they make it more profound, since they enforce 'truth' from every point of view. Now, a true symbol, in a sense, or from a certain point of view, *is* what it symbolizes and architectural symbolism corresponds to this ideal almost by necessity.

2. GOPURAMS: THE GATES

Returning now to the Shri Minakshi Sundareswar, the temple built on its sacred ground *is*, in relation to the profane world, what it symbolizes, namely the realm of non-gross manifestation in relationship to the gross.[18] This symbolism establishes a marked discontinuity between what is gross and what is non-gross and the temple's perimeter is the line of demarcation between the different orders of manifestation. There must be, however, contact between these realms to enable the being to pass from the lower into the higher ones; this passage, as we have seen in the personified symbol of Ganesha, cannot occur indiscriminately without certain restrictions and limiting conditions.

The perimeter of the Shri Minakshi Sundareswar is a huge square[19] solidly walled in; the demarcation, according to our cyclic conditions, is emphatic indeed and the 'points of contact' to permit the 'beginning' of the passage from the lower to the higher states of the being are restricted to the four gate towers or Gopurams[20] facing the four cardinal directions (Pl. 2a). These enormous Gopurams are the embodiment of the ever-increasing importance of the transition between the gross and the non-gross; they are by far the most dominant of all the structures in the whole of the Great Temple; and their overwhelming nature from a strictly compositional and structural point of view is so striking[21] that their symbolism needs further elucidation.

The rigorous correspondence between architectural symbol and 'architectural fact', springs here to light with crystalline clarity: the symbol for the point of contact between the gross and non-gross is the gate, which, in the corporeal world of forms, *is* the point of contact between outside and inside. The Gopurams mark the point physically for the passage from the profane to the sacred and mentally, from preoccupations directed towards material to those directed towards spiritual ends. Much the same way as the worshipper has to 'pass through' Ganesha by propitiating him and only after having 'praised and worshipped' him can the progress to the 'higher gods' be continued, the Gopuram of the temple has to be passed through, 'admired and experienced', before the sacred ground would be reached. Entering the gate to the sacred ground is the beginning of the sacrifice; and Ganesha is worshipped before every sacrifice. Parvati ordered him 'to keep strict guard at her gate'; in this sense Ganesha becomes the personified aspect governing the act of the entry, just as the Gopuram is its architectural symbol. Moreover, the gate is in a physical sense an obstacle, because by its very existence it restricts passages from all possible directions to a selected few, but at the same time, it is the removal of the obstacle because by it and by it alone is the access opened from the profane to the sacred. As a physical fact the gate is an opening, but an opening that can easily be locked; as a symbol the gate is the 'opening' which stands ajar and only for those qualified to enter the higher states of the being. In the open position the gate invites entry, much the same way as Ganesha urges on with his goad; in the locked position the gate bars entry, much the same way as Ganesha withholds with his lassoo.

These parallel analogies have been developed – and far from exhaustively at that – to show that the architectural symbol of the gate is no different from the personified and iconographic symbol of Ganesha. The Gopuram and Ganesha, in their necessarily different form since they are expressed by different forms of art, are equivalent symbols of the same principle; the enormous 'popularity' of Ganesha amongst millions of Hindus and the enormous mass and detail lavished on the Gopurams are further correspondences showing the ever-increasing relative importance of the principle which governs the 'state of transition' from the gross to the higher orders of manifestation.

The Hindus of the Shaivite tradition worship Ganesha in two different aspects. All of them worship him as an intermediary who opens access to Parvati, Shiva or other personified aspects of *Ishwara*, the Lord of Universal Being. Some and not a few, worship Ganesha as their personal god, that is, they worship *Ishwara* solely through the aspects which Ganesha personifies. In the latter case Ganesha's importance is, of course, vastly increased. Instead of being just the 'son' and 'gatekeeper', he becomes the 'anointed' and as such the personified symbol of the 'impersonal and therefore absolutely Universal Principle' which is approached and worshipped through the aspects embodied in him.

The parallel analogy of this happening in architecture is simply this: the gate becomes the symbol of the temple, or, in other words, the whole of the temple becomes symbolically externalized in the gate. This structure, then, necessarily develops 'out of proportion' of its former state and becomes in both mass and detail a towering symbol, which the Gopurams of the Shri Minakshi Sundareswar in fact are.

* * *

The elevation of the Gopuram with the adjoining temple wall, as it reveals itself to the external world, infers emphatically the fundamental juxtapositioning of the horizontal and the vertical direction (Pl. 2b). The temple wall, stretching on the south elevation approximately 850 ft., lined with trees, shrubs and forming the surrounding street alignment in an almost never-beginning-never-ending way, is the 'connection' between the town, the 'outside' and the temple, the 'inside' (Pl. 2c). This connection, which corresponds to the horizontal direction, the 'earth-hugging' aspect, therefore to the Earth, Substance, *Prakriti*, is so unobtrusive and mellow, so unpretentious and integrated, that one is hardly aware of the existence of a huge temple beyond, were it not for the tremendous rising verticality of the Gopurams, affirming, with full force, the opposite aspect, the Sky, Essence, *Purusha*; the intersection of these two directions, the horizontal and the vertical – or in other words, the coincidence of the two aspects, the essential and the substantial – marks the door, the point and the only point on this elevation which is different from all other points simply because it *is* the 'intersection' or the 'coincidence'. It symbolically corresponds to the internal centre of the temple, externalized and elevated towards the outside; it becomes thus the natural symbol of the total temple, the ground plan of which expresses no less formidably the same symbolism on the

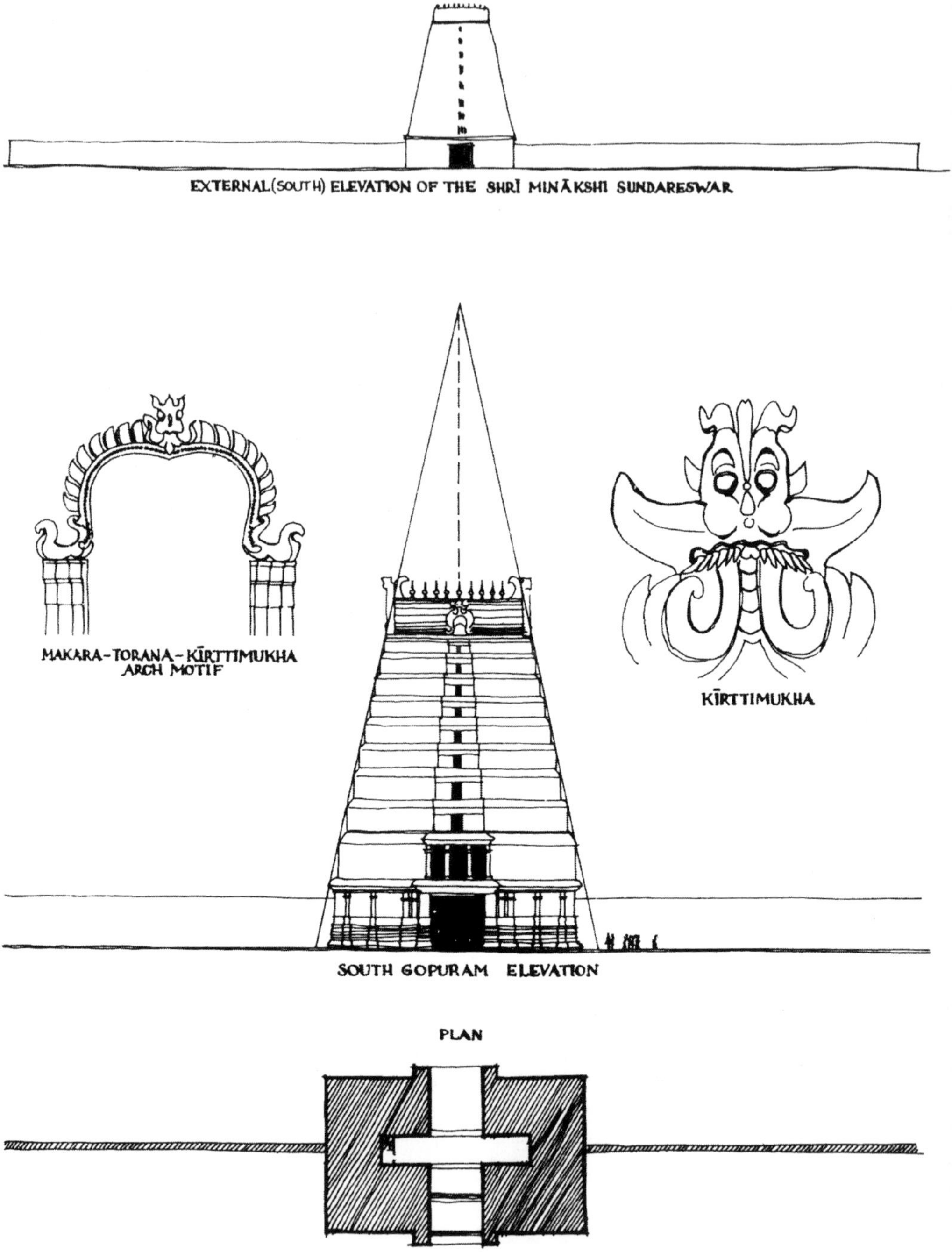

Fig. 1. Elevation of the Gopuram and the *Makara-Torana-Kirttimukha* motif

horizontal plane.[22] Whatever is then the centre on the horizontal plane, it corresponds to the door on the vertical plane and the structure rising above the door corresponds, even according to simple geometrical analogy, to the structure extended around the temple's core. The Gopuram is therefore symbolically equivalent to the whole of the temple from the architectural point of view as well.[23]

The plan of the Gopuram is a rectangle and over this rectangle is erected a truncated pyramid, presenting to all cardinal directions a triangle, the summit of which, due to its truncated form, is, so to speak, invisible (Fig. 1). This enormous mass is differentiated in the vertical as well as in the horizontal direction; the sides facing the outside and the inside of the temple are broken into three parts, the central portion projecting beyond the plane of the right and left (Pl. 3). This projecting mass rises directly above the door, accentuating the 'central nature' of the opening. In the vertical sense, the Gopurams are divided into a number of tiers or 'levels', varying in number according to the structure's total height. Each of the levels recedes above the one below and forms thereby the inward-leaning sides of the triangles mentioned before. Within the projecting central portion openings are formed at each level, situated directly above the entrance door, to which they correspond. All visible surfaces of the tiers, projections and sides are profusely covered with sculpture of teeming richness, differentiating, in a successive, hierarchical descent, the enormous total mass to the scale of a human hand. The significance of the details of these beautiful and awe-inspiring structures are far-reaching indeed.

The general symbolism inherent in the triangle is that of the Triad of Manifestation.[24] The case of a triangle placed with its summit on the top and its base at the bottom, which is the case at the Gopurams, involves 'a first principle (at least in a relative sense) from which two opposite, or rather complementary terms derive'.[25] The summit corresponding to a first principle, the two corners at the base to the two complementary terms, namely 'to universal Essence and Substance issued from a polarization of Being or of principial Unity'.[26] These latter terms in the Hindu tradition are called *Purusha* and *Prakriti*, the first pair of opposites of manifestation, issued from *Ishwara*, who is the Lord or Principle of universal manifestation, Itself unmanifest. The 'right' and 'left' corners of the base correspond to *Purusha* and *Prakriti*; the summit, its projection on the plan and the axis connecting these two points is the 'Centre' and corresponds to *Ishwara*. The facade of the Gopuram symbolizes all this in a perfectly coherent manner, since it differentiates by the projection of its central portion between the terms 'Centre', 'right' and 'left'. The truncated nature of the triangle, referred to before, might thus be taken to symbolize the invisible and therefore 'inexpressible' summit of the triangle corresponding to pure Being, 'inexpressible' on account of being unmanifest.[27]

The central axis which connects the invisible summit to the centre of the base carries in itself, as a continuous projection, the symbolic content of the summit. From this aspect the summit is projected upon the ground as the door, placed centrally between 'right' and 'left' and is equivalent to the 'Centre' from one point of view and to the summit of the triangle from another. Moreover, this relationship established on the ground level – that is on the level of the 'earth', or gross manifestation – appears similarly on the higher levels of the tiers, that is on the levels above gross manifestation. It is represented at every level no longer as a door in the physical sense, but simply as an 'opening', affirming that the non-gross states of manifestation relate in exactly the same way to the 'Centre' as the gross state does, being subject in exactly the same way to 'right' and 'left' opposition caused from the derivation of universal Essence and Substance, which apply, precisely because of their universality, to all manifested states.

One will have to guard here against a possible misunderstanding which may imply a contradiction in all that has been said before. On the one hand it has been established that the relationship between the horizontal perimeter of the temple and the vertical mass of the Gopuram corresponds to Substance and Essence respectively; on the other hand, the symbolism inherent in the triangle shows that the Gopuram itself is symbolic, not merely of both Essence and Substance but in addition of universal Being from which Essence and Substance derive. All seeming contradiction, however, will disappear if it is understood that the point of view from which these two different correspondences have been developed has changed; the former case took one elevation of the temple as a whole, the latter case the Gopuram by itself. These two points of view can be understood also in a purely physical sense, involving a distance long enough in the first case to view the temple as a whole and a distance much shorter in the second case enabling the observation of the Gopuram from much closer quarters. All this is perfectly valid from an architectural point of view, this being yet another instance showing the rigorous correspondence between architectural symbolism and 'architectural fact'. Due to the long distance separating the observer from the temple in the first case, the Gopuram appears simply as a vertical mass and its detail is lost for the observer as long as the distance is not reduced. Only by reducing this distance will the Gopuram be 'rediscovered' in a much more telling way and it is only then that its major and minor subdivisions become visible and comprehensible. Moreover, the two points of view are mutually exclusive since the detail is visible only from a point from which the total perspective is necessarily lost.[28]

Yet there exists an even closer point of view which brings into sharp focus the surface detailing of the horizontal tiers (Pl. 4a). These levels are situated above the plane of physical communication and refer to the orders of manifestation beyond the gross; they are profusely covered with symbolic sculpture and iconography representing the personified gods and their hosts, the myths of the *Puranas*, deities (*Devas*) and demons (*Asuras*) of all order and status in such an abounding, never-repeating procession that to consider them individually is obviously beyond our scope. In their collectivity, however, they bring home strikingly the notion that however vast the extension of gross manifestation may be, it is superseded by far by the truly unfathomable indefinity of the non-gross states of manifestation. But what is perhaps even more baffling about the excellence of this architectural symbol taken as a whole is that, instead of losing itself in the almost incalculable multiplicity of forms, it gains a unity hitherto unexperienced. This Unity is quite different from the arithmetic or quantitative 'units' which are simply contained in multiplicity without being referred to any higher principle. A multiplicity of this kind is 'purely quantitative, it could be said to be quantity itself, deprived of all quality; on the other hand, the multiplicity of the higher order, or that which can be so called analogically, is really a qualitative multiplicity, that is to say the integrality of the qualities and attributes which constitute the essence of beings and of things'.[29] This latter kind of multiplicity, which is contained in metaphysical Unity, is none other than the indefinitely numerous attributes of God Himself and it is precisely this that the incalculable iconographical variety fused into the majestic Unity of the Gopurams of the Shri Minakshi Sundareswar temple symbolizes (Pl. 4b).

3. THE FACE OF GLORY

The truncated pyramid of the Gopuram is completed by a barrel-vaulted roof form; affixed to the four sides of this roof facing the four cardinal directions is the crowning motif of the whole structure, the *Kirttimukha* or 'Face of Glory'. With these formal elements of great significance the symbolism of the Gopuram is fulfilled (Pls. 5, 6).

The super-position of a barrel-vaulted roof over a rectangular base or of a dome over a square chamber is the architectural solution inevitably adopted over the central shrine of the Hindu temple. The Gopuram, however, as indicated before, is the symbolic equivalent of the total temple and thus it is easily seen that the origin and meaning of the barrel-vaulted roof, which crowns the truncated pyramid, must be traced back to the dome-form covering the central shrine.

This theme has very deep and far-reaching significance and will be developed fully in the last part of this study when it will be established why the central shrine 'is *obliged* to forsake its plan and strain forward to meet the round dome in which it must terminate.'[30] One may just briefly allude here to 'the sides of a pyramid contracting towards a common point in which their independent existence ceases[31]', which form involves the same notion, that is the fundamental procedure from quadrature to unity. The 'common point' in the case of the Gopuram's truncated form is 'invisible', yet it is virtually present in the apex of the barrel-vault where the rising faces of the structure terminate. This termination of the quadrature in unity, however, does not represent absolute finality in the Hindu tradition, since the vault, by which the termination is achieved, is pierced by 'axes', 'arrows' or 'shafts' which break through and go beyond the apparent completeness of the cover (Pl. 5). The significance of all this will be considered later in the symbolism of the dome.

However, it is possible right now to conceive of the cross-section of a dome or of the end elevation of the barrel-vault, as the projection of a three-dimensional form upon a two-dimensional plane: this line will trace, in fact, the form of an arch over an opening. The two-dimensional projection of a three-dimensional form represents a reduction in dimensions; the unification of the quadrature inherent in the dome becomes, analogically, the unification of duality inherent in the arch. The arch, whether flat or raised, is an indispensable structural element to forming an opening in masonry constructions. The Gopuram *is* a gate – an opening – and involves necessarily the use of the arch-form constructionally, structurally as well as symbolically. In fact, the arch-motif crowning the Gopuram as the *Kirttimukha* is by no means the only place where this motif appears; it appears over every single opening and niche of this immense structure, too numerous to count (Pl. 4a). It seems, then, quite appropriate to reflect upon the arch-motif at length here and to bring thereby to a close the reflections on the symbolism of the Gopuram.

In the Hindu arch-motif one can distinguish three major elements: first the two *Makaras*, or sea-monsters, placed at the two springing points; second, the *Torana*, or arch-line itself; and third, the *Kirttimukha*, or Face of Glory, corresponding to the apex of the arch (Fig. 1). In order to develop the integral significance of the three major elements fully it will be necessary to examine them first separately in some detail.[32]

The *Makara* is a monster with pronounced aquatic nature; mostly it resembles the form of the crocodile, but it assumes quite often the characteristics of the elephant and also of the fish. Very often it is the combination of all these zoological forms, unrecognizable as a specimen but a fusion or confusion of its prototypes.[33] 'It may be remarked at once, that as a great Leviathan moving in the waters, the *Makara* is obviously the symbol of the waters; and as it will appear from its associations, more specifically of the Essence in the Waters, the principle of life.'[34] '*Rasa*, as Essence in the Waters, or as sap in the trees, is variously identified with Soma, *Amrita*, semen, milk, honey, mead (*madhu*) and liquor (*sura*); there is a cycle in which the vital energy passes from heaven through the waters, plants, cattle and other typically virile or productive animals and man, thence ultimately returning to the waters.'[35] There is undoubtedly something obscure about this sea-monster, as the *obscure origin of life*, as the 'Essence in the Waters', since this 'Essence' must on no account be confused with universal Essentiality, but understood rather as its effect, mirrored or imagined, upon universal Substantiality, 'in which nothing is distinguished or actualized'[36] and therefore necessarily obscure and unintelligible. 'Darkness there was at first, enveloped in darkness; without distinctive marks all this was water. That which was void and wrapped in a husk, that One by power of heat (*tapas*) came into being.'[37]

In plant-symbolism 'the lotus is the waters'[38] and the connection between *Makara* and lotus, both in appearance and in nature, has been convincingly documented.[39] The parvan or the node of the lotus-rhizome is the symbolic equivalent of the *Makara*; just as the parvan is the point of emergence of the lotus stem, the jaws of the *Makara* serve as the point of origin of the *Torana-arch*, which is therefore of vegetative character in the first place.[40] Generally speaking, it is the *growth* which originates in the 'Essence of the Waters', the result of the 'principle of life', that is, it is life itself in its superabundance and incalculable variety, making up the whole of the manifested world.

From its origin, which is the *Makara*, the *Torana-arch* symbolically unfolds all the facets of existence until it reaches the apex of the arch, the 'common point' of right and left, where the 'independent existence' of the two sides ceases. It is precisely at this point, at this 'key' that the *Kirttimukha*, the third and most important, item of the arch-motif is placed.

For the origin of the *Kirttimukha* we turn again to the texts of the *Skanda-purana* :[41]

There was once a great titan king called Jalandhara. By virtue of extraordinary austerities he had accumulated to himself irresistible powers. Equipped with these, he had gone forth against the gods of all the created spheres and, unseating them, had established his new order. His humiliating government was tyrannical, wasteful, careless of the traditional laws of the universe, wicked and utterly selfish. In a tremendous and ultimate excess of pride, Jalandhara sent a messenger-demon to challenge and humble the High-God himself, Shiva the creator, sustainer and destroyer of the world. The challenge brought by the messenger Rahu was that Shiva should give up his shining jewel of a bride, 'The Fairest Maiden of All Worlds' and without further ado turn her over to the new master of existence, the titan tyrant, Jalandhara.

The moment Rahu tendered Jalandhara's demand that the Goddess should be delivered to him – the *Shakti* of the universe to become the tyrant's principal queen – Shiva countered the colossal challenge. From the spot between his two eyebrows – the spot called the 'Lotus of Command' (*Ajna-Chakra*) where the centre of enlightenment is located and the spiritual eye of the advanced seer is opened – the god let fly a terrific burst of power, which explosion immediately took the physical shape of a horrendous, lion-headed demon. The alarming body of the monster was lean and emaciated, giving notice of insatiable hunger, yet its strength was resilient and obviously irresistible. The apparition's throat roared like thunder; the eyes burnt like fire; the mane, dishevelled, spread far and wide into space. Rahu was aghast.

When the incarnate burst-of-wrath made a rush at the blasphemous demon-messenger, Rahu, in his terrific fright took refuge in the all-protecting fatherhood and benevolence of the Almighty, Shiva himself. The god immediately bade the monster to spare the petitioner and the half-lion was left with a painful hunger but no proper food on which to feast it. The creature asked the God to assign some victim on which the torment might be appeased.

Shiva suggested that the monster should feed on the flesh of its own feet and hands. Forthwith, that incredible incarnation of blind voraciousness proceeded to satiate its congenital hunger. And having devoured not only its feet and hands, but its legs and arms as well, it was still unable to stop. The teeth went on through its own belly and chest and neck, until only the face remained.

Shiva watched silently, but with supreme delight, the blood-curdling, nightmarish procedure and then, gratified by the vivid manifestation of the self-consuming power of his own substance, he smiled upon that creature of his wrath – which had reduced its own body, joint by joint, to the nothingness of only a face – and benignantly declared: 'You will be known, henceforth, as Face of Glory (*Kirttimukha*) and I ordain that you shall abide forever at my door. Whosoever neglects to worship you shall never win my grace.

This Puranic myth is certainly not lacking in motifs and allusions profoundly disturbing to the western mind. Unlike the Hindus, the western mentality has become accustomed to view its gods as all-fatherly and benevolent, relegating the concept of evil to the fallen angels and 'adversaries', who in the personified form of the Devil become solely malevolent and infernal. The Hindu tradition, however, has preserved the essential unity of the principle superordinate to the duality of good and evil; and Shiva in this instance, as well as in innumerable other cases, reasserts this principle in no uncertain terms. Rahu, the blasphemous messenger of the titan-tyrant, gains instantaneous 'salvation', having abandoned all sacrilegious claims in his primordial terror, whereas the lion-faced 'burst of wrath', a production of Shiva himself, is perpetuated after having almost completely devoured itself. His 'insatiable, congenital hunger', however, remains unappeased and it is in this form that the *Kirttimukha* keeps on devouring, as the top-piece of the arch-motif, the manifested world. Whatever gains existence from the obscure 'principle of life' in the waters, nourished in the tenebrous womb and issued from the jaws of the *Makaras*, climbs the *Torana*-arch of life only to be devoured by Face of Glory at the top. The Face of Glory is then certainly not the 'glory of life', since it is precisely this glory of life which is Jalandhara's abominable challenge to Shiva in his 'tremendous and ultimate excess of pride', for 'the Fairest Maiden of All Worlds', which is in other words the 'Ground of Universal Manifestation'; this claim is countered by Shiva's 'terrific burst of power' 'in the shape of a horrendous lion-headed demon' of which, eventually, the devouring Face of Glory alone remains. The Face of Glory, then, is indeed the 'glory of transformation', the glory of the world *beyond* the false glory of life. Devouring is here equivalent to transformation from the lower to the higher states of the being and it is this transformation which the *Kirttimukha*, as Shiva's particular aspect, but *a fortiori* Shiva as the Transformer, symbolizes.

The arch-motif of the *Makara-Torana-Kirttimukha* triad is then the symbol of the endless cycles of manifestation (*Samsara*); eminently real as long as it is viewed from within manifestation itself, but eminently unreal once viewed from a position outside it. The 'bonds of Varuna', whose reign is the waters, are the same as the 'bonds of the *Makaras*' and the 'bonds of life' which issue from the jaws of the *Makaras*. These bonds can only be loosened by the *Kirttimukha*, the 'all-devourer' and only through the terrible transformation caused by its insatiable hunger will the glory of the boundless state be revealed, the same glory of which the Face of Glory is the gate.[42]

It remains now to establish the relation of the *Makara-Torana-Kirttimukha* symbol with the arch-form considered strictly in an architectural sense. From this point of view the arch, whether flat or raised, is the connection of the two sides of an opening, without which no opening can be conceived, nor constructed. In masonry constructions its raised form originates at the 'springing line' or more specifically at the right and left springing point and tracing a curved line of some kind, converges from both sides towards the centre line of the opening; it is at the central line, which coincides with the apex of the arch, that the convergence ceases, that the arch becomes complete and that in certain particular modes of construction it receives its 'key'.[43]

The foregoing description of the arch establishes in the verbal mode its formal and structural meaning which is identical with the iconography of the *Makara-Torana-Kirttimukha* symbol. The support of the arch is below its springing line, just as the 'support' of manifestation is 'the Waters' or 'substance', which from the Latin sub-stare is, in fact, support. The 'springing line' or the right and left 'springing point', coincides with the right and left *Makara*, the 'principle of life' from which life springs into being or, in other words, from which the lotus-stem of the *Torana* issues; the converging arc *is* the arch itself; the structural form which 'does the work' and develops the stresses, just as the *Torana* develops the facets of manifestation, the path of life. The arc completes itself at the centre line and it is there that it 'ceases to exist'; and receives its meaning and indispensable structural 'key' – much the same way as the *Torana* motif of manifested existence 'receives its meaning' by being devoured in the *Kirttimukha.*

From another point of view the apex of the arch is the 'common point' of the right and left arc and in this sense it is no different from the apex of the triangle referred to before. It is the common source of two complementary principles, which in this case may be identified with the right and left springing point; the source of the two complementary principles is the principle of Being, in which all separate aspects of existence cease and are equally 'devoured', whether this 'separateness' is conceived on the macrocosmic scale of the manifested worlds[44] or on the microcosmic scale of the human individual.

It is then only by being devoured that the centre, 'the spot between Shiva's two eyebrows', is reached and it is only by giving up his separate existence that 'the spiritual eye of the advanced seer is opened'. The terrifying Face of Glory, upheld to the four cardinal directions on the top of the Gopurams, is then really the 'gate', through which the road of the spiritual seeker to the elevated realms inevitably leads.

NOTES AND REFERENCES

1. The Hindu cyclic theory of time surpasses in its scale vastly the western concepts and is based on periodical creations and dissolutions. Every creator, Brahma, is given 100 god-years after which he is absorbed into *Ishwara* and after a period of non-manifestation a new Brahma arises. At the end of every day of each Brahma all existence is absorbed into the night of Brahma: this period is called a single *Kalpa,* 1 *Kalpa* = 14 *Manvantaras* = 1000 *Mahayugas* = 4000 *Yugas* = 4,32,00,00,000 human years. Each *Kalpa* has a different name. The present *Kalpa* is *Varaha Kalpa.* For a fuller explanation see A.K. Coomaraswamy, *Myths of the Hindus and Buddhists,* p. 392.
2. Gatekeeper.
3. Shiva-*Purana,* quoted according to T.A. Gopinatha Rao, *Elements of Hindu Iconography,* Madras, 1914, p. 36.
4. *Ibid.,* p. 43.
5. Somanatha was the place of a sacred shrine dedicated to Shiva. The *Purana* relates that whoever visited this shrine at a certain period was miraculously elevated to the abode of gods.
6. *Skanda Purana,* according to T.A. Gopinatha Rao, *op.cit.,* p. 43.
7. Parvati as the symbol of Substantiality – just as Shiva, the symbol of Essentiality and as Brahma, the Supreme Principle – has a supreme (*Para*) and non-supreme (*Apara*) aspects. *Para*-Brahma is the unqualified (*Nirguna*), impersonal Supreme Principle; *Apara*-Brahma is the qualified (*Saguna*), personal Principle – Divine Personality – and

as such coincident with *Ishwara*, the Principle of Universal Being. The supreme (*Para*) aspect of Shiva as Universal Essentiality and of Parvati as Universal Substantiality may, from a special point of view, coincide symbolically with *Para*-Brahma that is, it may represent the Principle of manifestation and non-manifestation alike. (See also René Guénon, *Man and His Becoming*, *op.cit.*, pp. 80-86 and notes.)

8. The metaphysical theory of inverse analogy connecting the principial and manifested orders is expanded generally in the works of René Guénon. The understanding of this theory lies in the conceiving of the manifested world as the mirror image of the principial order. 'In consequence of this analogy the highest realities are most clearly manifested in their remotest reflections' (Frithjof Schuon, *The Transcendent Unity of Religions*, Faber and Faber, London, 1953, p. 81). 'That which is below is like that which is above and that which is above is like that which is below' (from the Emerald Table of the Hermetic tradition according to René Guénon, *Man and His Becoming*, *op.cit.*, p. 19).
9. Heinrich Zimmer, *Myths and Symbols in Indian Art and Civilization*, Bollingen Series VI, Pantheon Books Inc., New York, 1946, pp. 27-53.
10. The Hindu tradition recognizes five elements (*Bhutas*) from which the whole of gross or corporeal manifestation is made up. These are : Ether (*Akasha*), Air (*Vayu*), Fire (*Tejas*), Water (*Ap*), Earth (*Prithivi*). Needless to say that these 'elementary substances' are conceived in quite a different sense from the 'elements' of modern analytical chemistry and are incomparable to the latter as such.
11. The symbolism inherent in the animal-vehicles of the Hindu gods is far too extensive to treat here fully. Briefly, the rider corresponds to the higher aspects of the principle involved, the vehicle to the lower. Shiva's vehicle is the bull (Nandi), Parvati's the lion, Ganesha's the rat, Murugan's the peacock, Brahma's the swan and Vishnu's the boar.
12. Stella Kramrisch, *The Hindu Temple*, University of Calcutta, 1946, Vol. I, pp. 1-17.
13. This concept is diametrically opposed to that of the various forms of modern churches in the West, which are primarily built for the use of the congregation. The Hindu temple is abandoned – regardless of its size and splendour – once the Divine Presence withdraws.
14. An alternative expression would be 'visual' or 'plastic' art, but both these suffer from a lack of precision. What is meant here are those forms of art which are 'embedded' into static material, or to be even more precise, which rely upon the mineral and vegetative states of corporeal manifestation as their 'support' to become comprehensible to man.
15. The conditions here referred to are more specific than conditions governing corporeal manifestation in general, since they refer to the physical and biological make-up and functioning of the human body, which is a specific case within corporeal manifestation.

    The only condition – or law – that sculpture and painting cannot bypass in this respect is the law of vision. Here is then another reason why the reference to architecture as 'visual art' is incorrect, since this term, if used at all, can apply to sculpture, painting and the like only.
16. This qualification which is 'natural' to architecture has been, in recent times, falsely claimed by profane sculpture and painting with the introduction of pseudo-spatial concepts which belie the true character of these arts and which were never incorporated into the sacred forms of these arts.

17. Ganesha's iconographical symbol – elephant head on human body – does not correspond to the laws of gross manifestation. The very nature of architecture renders such symbolism impossible in architectural terms.
18. The Hindu tradition speaks of several orders of manifestation of which the physical, sensible, or gross is the lowest. The higher orders, which at this state are referred to simply as non-gross, or beyond gross, will be encountered in the second part of this study.
19. 852 ft. x 729 ft. approximately.
20. There is a fifth entrance not marked by a Gopuram on the perimeter: its hidden, almost secret nature will receive more attention in the second part of this study.
21. The highest Gopuram is 152 ft. high, rising above a base 110 ft. x 58 ft. approximately.
22. This symbolism will be fully developed in the last part of this study.
23. According to Titus Burckhardt, the temple as a whole is the door from terrestrial existence to higher levels of existence : the foregoing discussion showed that the door is the temple, which is its inverse equivalent.
24. The symbolism of the triangle is general in a sense that it transgresses the limits of the Hindu tradition and applies probably to all traditions of the human race. Cf. René Guénon , La Grande Triade (Revue de La Table Ronde, Paris, 1946), p. 20.
25. '...un principe premier (au moins en un sens relatif) dont dérivent deux terms opposés, ou plutôt complémentaires'. *Ibid.*
26. 'de l'Esence et de la Substance universelles, issues d'une polarisation de l'Etre ou de l'Unité principlielle...' *Ibid.*, p. 22.
27. One will recall here the temples of Nepal and China which are similarly inscribed into a pyramid, not 'reaching', however, in building form, the summit and thus leaving the 'point' invisible.
28. Traditional symbolism always adapts itself to such various relative points of view revealing various relative aspects of the Inexpressible. This is, furthermore, true not only in forms of representative art but also in forms of language and of thought conveying metaphysical truths. One could almost say that, without assuming the relativity of a given point of view, symbolism would be non-existent, since it refers by manifested forms to the Unmanifest; this would be an impossibility from an absolute point of view, since universal manifestation is strictly speaking nil compared to the Infinity of the Supreme Principle. The notion of the relativity of any point of view is fundamental to symbolism in general and this notion is expressed nowhere clearer than in architecture: due to its intimate relation with the human being it is capable of transposing metaphysical truths as simple 'facts' even into the corporeal or sensible world.
29. René Guénon, *The Reign of Quantity*, *op.cit.*, p. 18. As a telling contrast it is interesting to compare the structures of the present period in relation to what has just been said about the Gopuram. A tall city office building is often related in mass and scale to its surroundings in a manner that is not dissimilar to that of the Gopurams. What is radically different, however, is that it consists of 'endless' repetition of 'units' in a horizontal as well as in a vertical direction; and this modular repetition, referred to no higher principle, produces the kind of multiplicity devoid of any quality. Of course, these 'office buildings' serve the 'god' of quantity, Mammon and in this sense, architecture cannot help being what it is and is thus, to a certain extent, incorruptible.
30. E. Schroeder, *Survey of Persian Art*, according to A.K. Coomaraswamy.

31. A.K. Coomaraswamy, Symbolism of the Dome, *The Indian Historical Quarterly*, Vol. XIV, No. I, March 1938, p. 2.
32. The *Makara-Torana-Kirttimukha* motif appears throughout the East in countless number of cases and variations defying any imagination. Not only is it spread through the regions under Hindu and later Buddhist influence, which includes Tibet, Nepal, Southeast Asia, Indonesia, China and Japan, but it appears in modified form even in the art of Islam and, more curious still, in the Christian West, admittedly in isolated cases.

    The historical origin of the *Makara* is probably the most remote, that of the *Kirttimukha* less so; and their combination in the arch-motif is the latest. Nevertheless, it is in this combination that the amazing spread of the elements occurred, because it is in this combination that they have found their proper place, their meaning supported and reinforced by the correspondences inherent in the architectural form of the arch.
33. F.D.K. Bosch, *The Golden Germ, An Introduction to Indian Symbolism*, Mouton & Co., The Hague, 1960, pp. 1-23.
34. A.K. Coomaraswamy, *Yakshas*, Part II, Washington, D.C., 1931, p. 47.
35. *Ibid.*, p. 25.
36. René Guénon, *The Reign of Quantity*, *op.cit.*, p. 25.
37. *Rig-Veda*, X. 129, 3, according to Bosch, *op.cit.*
38. Bosch, *op.cit.*, pp. 23-51.
39. Bosch, *op.cit.*, pp. 1-51.
40. It would take us too far to discuss here the almost endless variations which can be applied to the *Torana*-arch in which the vegetative character is suppressed. Snakes, pearl-strings, human figures and animals, interlaced with vines, branches and leaves appear in many instances; in all these cases the form is interchangeable, but the symbolic content remains stable.
41. *Skanda-Purana*, Vol. II, *Vishnukanda, Karttikamasa Mahatmya*, Chapter 17, cf. Rupam I. (Calcutta, Jan. 1920), pp. 11-19. This passage is freely quoted according to Zimmer, *op.cit.*, p. 175.
42. In this connection it is interesting to recall the rock of Sigirya in Ceylon which rises almost vertically from the surrounding plains; it accommodated on the top a once glorious palace of which now the ruins only remain. Just to what extent has this edifice been constructed along traditional principles is difficult to assess at this stage, since excavations and research are still in progress. There are, however, sufficient signs to indicate its profound significance. What is relevant here is that the single passage, carved in almost unscalable rock, passed through an enormous lion-head before it emerged on the top.
43. From the general point of view it is of no significance whether the arch is vaulted or corbelled, whether it is homogeneous, monolithic, or made up of a number of separate items. The Hindus very rarely used vaulting and the Shri Minakshi Sundareswar is completely free from this kind of construction. It is not the method of construction which is under examination here but the form itself, since the significance of the form is independent from the method of construction, much the same way as the pattern of the internal stresses are dependent upon the form of the structure and not upon its construction. In this connection not even the 'flat arch' is an exception, denoted by the etymological route of the architrave.

44. From the cosmological point of view the symbolism of the arch is similarly extensive and will be touched upon only briefly here. The cosmological prototype of the arch is the arc of the sun as it traces its passage from sunrise to sunset. The third significant point is, of course, the zenith, the unique point which separates the rise from the fall. In this connection it is said that the sun 'rests at noon' on the apex of the arch and therefore, the apex of the arch is likened to the sun, the fiery element; and also to the *Vedic* god Agni (literally 'fire'), whose fiery and devouring nature is described in texts too numerous to quote here. It is similarly well known that the lion is the fiery element in the animal world and that the sun (Surya) is not merely the essential aspect of life but also the devourer of life. The *Kirttimukha*-Shiva-Agni-Surya-Lion aspects thus are interchangeable and correlative with respect to the top of the arch and with respect to the top of the dome, which symbolism will be developed more fully later.

PART II

BETWEEN BOUNDARY AND CENTRE

Taijasa, the seat of which is in the dream state, is U, the second *Matra*, because it is the elevation and also because it participates in both. He who knows this in truth advances along the path of Knowledge and he is in harmony and none of his descendants will be ignorant of Brahma.

Mandukya Upanishad
Shruti 10

1. CIRCUMAMBULATION

Unhindered by the guardians of the door and unopposed in his passage under the gate-tower the spiritual seeker 'advances along the path of Knowledge' towards the 'elevated' realms that are beyond the gross or sensible world. The hustle and bustle of the town are leftbehind, the atmosphere changes perceptibly, the mental attitude is becalmed and an unmistakable sense of 'being inside' prevails. One finds oneself in a domain which is intermediate between the 'outside' and the 'core'; and because it is intermediate it 'participates in both'. This is the 'interspace'[1] between the outer and the innermost wall, the realm of subtle or ideal manifestation[2] (Fig. 2).

A. Raya (East) Gopuram
B. Viravasantaraya *Mandapam*
C. Katyana-Sundara and Servaikaran *Mandapam*
D. Minakshi Nayaka *Mandapam*
E. *Ashta Shakti Mandapam*
F. Tiruvachi Gopuram
G. Open Square
H. South Gopuram
I. Minakshi *Prakaram* Gopuram (West)
J. Sundareswar *Prakaram* Gopuram (West)
K. West Gopuram
L. North Gopuram
M. Sundareswar *Prakaram* Gopuram (North)
N. Sabhapati or Sixteen Pillar *Mandapam*
O. Sahasrastambha or Thousand Pillar *Mandapam*
P. Shrine of Nateshwara
Q. Sundara Pandya Gopuram of Sundareswar *Prakaram* (East)
R. Nandi *Mandapam*, *Stambha* and *Vedi*
S. Aruvati Muvar and Nateshwara
T. Gopuram of the Shrine of Sundareswar
U. Gopuram between Minakshi and Sundareswar *Prakaram* (South)
V. Gopuram of the Minakshi *Prakaram* (East)
X. *Pottamarai Kulam* (the Tank of the Golden Lilies)
Y. Vimana of Lord Sundareswar
Z. Vimana of Shri Minakshi

The Hindu devotee traditionally circumambulates the inner sanctum instead of approaching it directly, so as to encounter the numerous edifices and iconographical representations that occur in the 'interspace'; they serve as his supports to facilitate the transition from the gross, which is left behind, to the formless, which is not yet encountered. It is best to adopt the same approach here and now to become familiar with the layout of this huge temple, a layout entirely incomprehensible from the outside since only four walls and four enormous Gopurams are visible externally.

Entering then (Fig. 2) the Eastern (Raya) Gopuram (A), the road leads to a roofed pillared hall, the Viravasantaraya *Mandapam* (B) in which various dealers ply their trade (Pl. 7a), affirming that the 'interspace' 'participates in both' the outside as well as the core. Diverging to the left at the third of the length of this *Mandapam* to follow the strictly observed clockwise direction of the circumambulation,[3] the subdued light of the pillared hall is changed for the open sky and a small square is reached in which two smaller halls, called Katyana-Sundara and Servaikaran *Mandapam* (C), find their place amongst tropical vegetation. Further on is the Minakshi Nayaka *Mandapam* (D) with six rows of pillars supporting the roof (Pl. 7b); here are the stalls of the elephants used at festivals and in processions. The central passage of this hall is in fact the second axial entrance from the east; the former originating at the Raya Gopuram (A) leads to the central shrine of Sundareswar, whereas this latter one originates at the small *Ashta-Shakti Mandapam* (E) and leads to the central shrine of Shri Minakshi. The *Ashta-Shakti Mandapam*, which takes the place of a gate-tower, is literally 'Eight-Goddess' *Mandapam*, so called of the eight statues of the goddess supporting the roof of the hall on either side. On the right of the gate is the image of Murugan, on the left Ganesha, the two sons of Minakshi and Sundareswar (Parvati and Shiva). The Tiruvachi Gopuram (F), which is the main 'gate' to the Shri Minakshi approach, rises at the western end of the Minakshi Nayaka *Mandapam* (D).[4]

Proceeding to the south a sunny square (G) is reached once more where the elephants are exercised and processions are assembled; numerous enclosures open from this square housing the various paraphernalia used at festival time during the processions.

The passage now tightens turning towards the west and leads under open sky to the South Gopuram (H) (Pl. 2a) and further to the west to the several offices, built against the outside wall, where the administration of this huge temple is carried out and the records are kept. Turning to the north at the corner the space widens and two smaller Gopurams (I, J) belonging to the Minakshi and Sundareswar *Prakaram* (enclosure) are encountered to the right (Pl. 7c) and the main gate of the West Gopuram (K) to the left (Pl. 7d). A number of small shrines to various deities are found in this area built against the outside wall. Turning east, the main North Gopuram (L) is situated on the left and a smaller Gopuram (M) belonging to the *Prakaram* of Sundareswar to the right. At the end of this passage 'a small shrine, dedicated to the god Sabhapati (N), is reached which occupies the space of sixteen columns, but it is not their number but their marvellous elaboration that makes

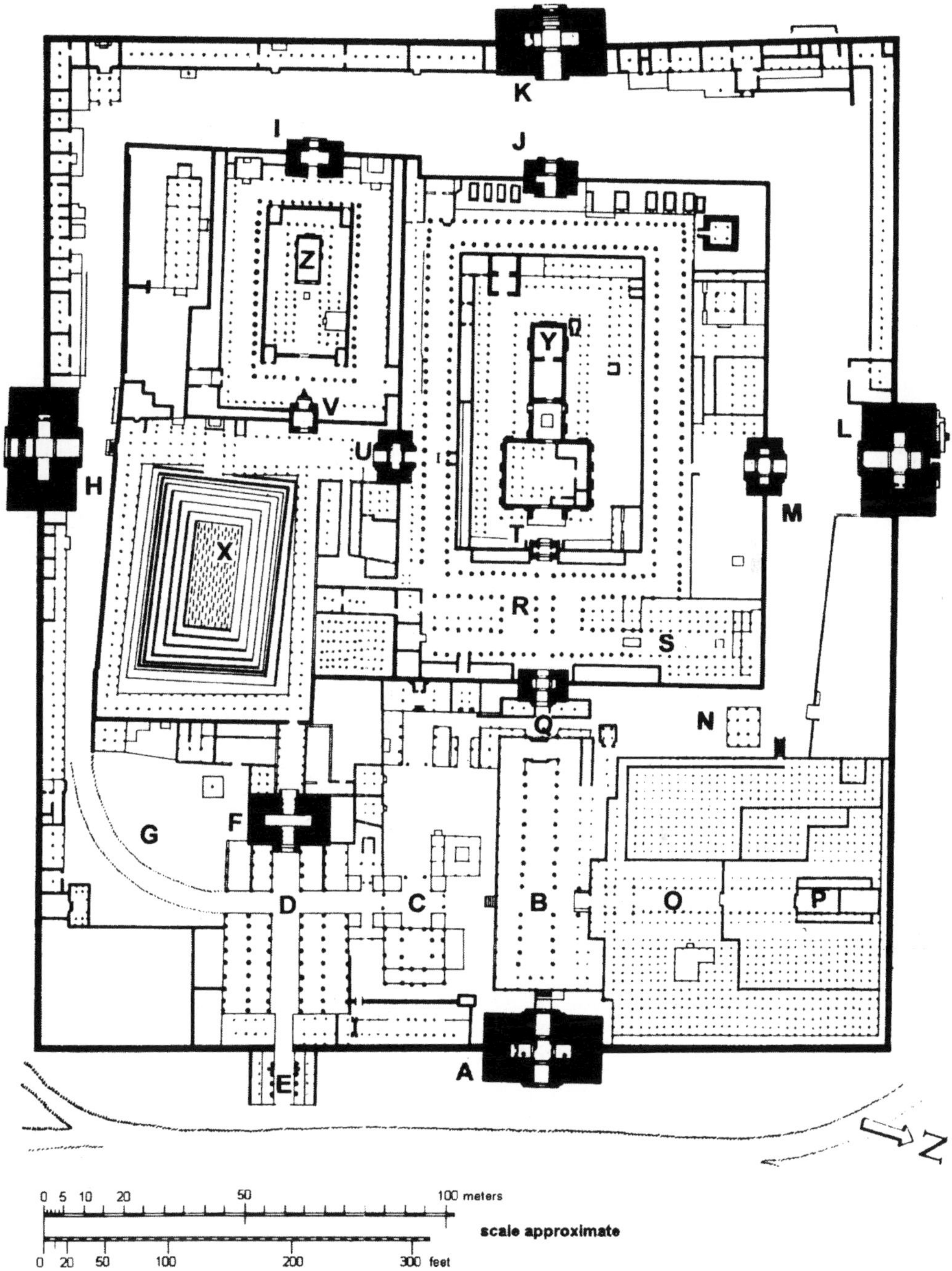

Fig. 2. Ground plan of the temple

it the wonder of this place'.[5] Immediately next to it, approachable also from the *Viravasantaraya Mandapam* (B) occupying a huge square (about 240 ft. x 240 ft.) is the 'Hall of Thousand Pillars' or *Sahasrastambha Mandapam* (O) (Pl. 7e). Most of the 997 pillars are differently carved and exhibit a profusion of iconographic symbolism; the main pillars in front of the shrine of Shiva as Nateshwara (P) have larger than life size sculptures of gods and goddesses, superbly carved (Pl. 8a). The hall is a masterpiece in handling dim light and shade in which the forest of vertical columns disappears into receding darkness in all directions. The atmosphere created defies any description: it has to be experienced to be understood.

The circumambulation of the outer circle being completed, the *Viravasantaraya Mandapam* (B) is reached once more with its noisy contrast of crowds of people and traders compared to the dim silence of the Hall of Thousand Pillars. Proceeding axially westward, after a brief period of blinding sunshine, the Sundara Pandya Gopuram (Q) leads to the enclosure (*Prakaram*) towards Sundareswar's central shrine (Pl. 8b). Immediately within, is a *Mandapam* of eight large and elaborately carved pillars (R), surrounding the *Vedi* or sacrificial altar, the *Stambha* or sacrificial post (Pl. 9) and the Nandi or bull, Shiva's vehicle, magnificently carved from monolithic granite (Pl. 10), facing with ever-ready devotion – yet supreme calm – to serve his Lord.

The interspace between the second and third wall is surrounded by a fine row of pillars supporting the roof in which raised lantern windows admit an evenly subdued light. Many small shrines and images of deities are found circumambulating this corridor; in the north-east corner eight steps are leading to the Aruvati Muvar, a large collection of statues of Hindu saints, the end of which is occupied once more by the image of Shiva as Nateshwara (S) (Pl. 11). The gate in front of Nandi (R) is the only gate leading to the third enclosure; it is the smallest Gopuram of all, through which no one but Hindus are allowed to pass (T). It leads to the most sacred shrine (Vimana or *Prasada*) of Sundareswar.

The atmosphere of the second enclosure is distinctly quiet and serene, the subdued light is even and soft; the sharp contrasts of brilliant light and blinding darkness encountered in the first enclosure are nowhere in evidence here. The only shaft of direct light bursts through from the ceiling over the *Nandi Mandapam* (R) which is pierced through by the sacrificial post (Pl. 9).

Passing once more behind the Nandi to the southern side, a Gopuram common to Minakshi and Sundareswar is reached (U) which leads to the *Prakaram* of Shri Minakshi. Immediately in front of and axial to the gate is a fine row of twelve pillars on either side of which are carved in the form of the strange fiery beast, the *Yali*, a fusion of horse and lion, depicted in the act of devouring a 'link' issued from a subdued beast situated between its hind legs (Pl. 12a, b, c). Between every two *Yalis* are the images of the five Pandava brothers of the epic of the *Mahabharata*, namely Yudhishthir, Arjun, Sahadeva, Nakula and Bhima, opposite Bhima being the sacrificial altar (*Vedi*) and the small Gopuram (V) to the Vimana or *Prasada* of Shri Minakshi; again only Hindus are allowed to pass. On the left side of the colonnade is the beautiful water tank, the *Teppa Kulam*, called *Pottamarai Kulam*, 'Tank of the Golden Lilies' (X). It is surrounded by a lovely arcade of typical South Indian pillars with lotus-bud capitals (Pl. 13) and a flight of steps by which the devotees descend to the water to bathe. Within the water a small square stone island is erected: on certain festival days the images of Minakshi and Sundareswar are installed there (Pl. 14a, b). The beautifully proportioned arcade, the scale and form of the descending steps, the reflecting surface of water, the vistas of tropical vegetation, of the surrounding Gopurams and the sunny sky make the Tank of the Golden Lilies a lovely enclosure with an intensely religious atmosphere (Pl. 15).

At the south-western corner of the surrounding arcade a small door leads directly to the South Gopuram (H) in which a small winding staircase links the several tiers from the ground to the top. Internally, all the tiers contain a simple, small, cross-shaped chamber, entirely bare; the light is admitted only through two small openings opposite each other, referred to before. From the top of the barrel-shaped roof breathtaking views reveal the extent of the temple and the town of Madura encircling the temple in all directions. The golden domes over the Vimana of Shri Minakshi (Z) and of Lord Sundareswar (Y) sparkle in the brilliant sunshine and the twelve Gopurams of successively diminishing height towards the centre are the only other vertical accents in the vast extent of horizontality. (Pl. 16, 17a).

Having circumambulated the temple in a traditional manner[6] it will now be appropriate to consider the seemingly complex architectural layout in an overall sense. Between the outer wall, with the four Gopurams facing the cardinal directions (A, H, K, L) and the next inner wall is the first enclosure, interspace or *Prakaram*. This space is common to and embraces both the Sundareswar and Minakhsi temples. The next wall surrounds two separate rectangular areas placed side by side: the temple of Shri Minakshi and the temple of Sundareswar. Each of these enclosures has minor Gopurams facing the cardinal directions and their number should be eight; actually, there are only six (F, I, J, M, Q, U) since one of them (U) is common to both temples and since the main South Gopuram (H) serves virtually as the southern Gopuram of the Shri Minakshi *Prakaram* on account of the restricted space.[7] Beyond these gates lies the second enclosure – obviously of a higher order, or of a more sacred character – but already separate for each of the two temples. The Sundareswar *Prakaram*, or second interspace, consists of colonnades and *Mandapams* roofed almost in their entirety encircling completely the third enclosure. The Shri Minakshi *Prakaram*, however, contains besides roofed colonnades the open *Pottamarai Kulam* (X) as well and embraces the third enclosure only virtually. The next, the third enclosure, has only one small Gopuram in both cases (T, V) leading to an even more sacred interspace which surrounds, now in both cases completely, the Vimana, the sanctum sanctorum of Lord Sundareswar (Y) and of Shri Minakshi (Z) respectively. The layout of the temple is thus quite clear: there are three enclosures to both sancta and there are four gates to each enclosure except to the innermost, which has only one. This basic layout leads to several important considerations.

2. PATTERNS OF THE VEDIC ALTAR

The origin[8] of the Hindu temple can be traced to the sacrifice, common to all traditions involving the use of the sacrificial altar (*Vedi*) upon which the offerings were burnt in the sacrificial fire (*Agni*). 'There is no indication or reference to temple in *Vedic* literature, but there is description of sacrificial altars which were used to be raised in the open air'.[9] The *Veda* speaks of this kind of sacrifice alone; there the square altar, the pillar of smoke rising from the sacrificial fire and the dome of the open sky above constituted the only geometrical symbolism. 'According to the *Rig-Veda* (X.90) it is *Purusha* whom the Devas sacrifice at the beginning of the cycle in order to form the various parts of the cosmos and the different types of living things...consequently every sacrifice in some way reproduces and compensates for the pre-temporal sacrifice of the Devas, in that the unity of total being is symbolically and spiritually reconstituted by the rite; the sacrificer is identified with the altar which he builds in the image of the universe and in accordance with the measurement of his own body; he is likewise identified with the sacrificial animal which replaces him by virtue of certain qualities; and finally his spirit is identified with the fire, which reintegrates the offering into the principial unlimitedness. Man, the altar, the holocaust and the fire are all *Prajapati* and He is the Divine Essence'.[10] 'The "golden man", a schematic representation of man which must be built into the altar with the head towards the East (the holocaust is always placed into this position) indicates the analogy between man and the sacrificial victim'.[11]

This, then, is the immutable principle upon which the Hindu temple, even in its present form, is based: a schematic representation of man must be built into the edifice.[12] 'This heightened significance of the human frame has been inherent in the consciousness of our (the Hindu) architects and the style of the structure they evolved has ample human references'.[13] 'One who probes into the significance of our (the Hindu) architectural terms will be struck by this conception of architecture in terms of the human organism'.[14]

The road from the archetypal form of the *Vedic* altar to the Great Temple at Madura – which, one could almost say, is the terminating point of several thousand years of Hindu temple building[15] – involved great changes even if the principle of the built-in human frame remained unaffected. In *Vedic* times anthropomorphic representation of the deities was out of the question and iconography or elaborate offerings to icons was not existent. The *Vedas*, as *Shruti*, however, 'exhibit only certain aspects of early Indian religion. Behind the pale of Aryan orthodoxy there lay an extensive and deep-rooted system and a decided tendency to anthropomorphic presentation'.[16] It is only in the later texts of second authority, the *Smriti*, but more specifically from the present point of view, in the Agamas and Tantras that iconographical representation is accepted.[17] The exact mode of transition from the direct sacrificial rites of *Vedic* times to the indirect ritual offerings of the age of the Agamas is no more possible to unravel; it is, however, beyond reasonable doubt that a roofed structure over the sanctum coincided with the use of images to which the offerings were made. Even so, 'in very early times the structure was simple and worship open and the main elements of a religious edifice seem to have been a basement (containing probably an altar or seat of the object of worship), columns, beams and roofing'.[18] In these times the building material was timber and due to the unstable character of this material no evidence of these early structures remains except for isolated instances.[19]

Under the *Tantric* system the rites and ceremonials connected with the Puja, the ritual offerings, became more and more elaborate, images were carved of gold and other precious metals studded with jewels of the most expensive kind and their iconography became more and more complex. This period[20] coincided with the transition from the unstable, light timber to the more stable, solid stone and the once open temple became gradually more enclosed with stone walls until the only communication of the sanctum with the external world consisted of a single door only. Nor did one wall suffice to protect the sanctum later: the *Vastu Shastras* speak of inner and outer walls and several further enclosures.[21] This brought about, of course, greatly extended dimensions and additional structures. All these influences then transformed the square *Vedic* altar, oriented with its four sides to the four cardinal directions into the huge, complex structure of the Shri Minakshi Sundareswar punctuated with four enormous Gopurams.

The causes underlying this astonishing change are far from being easily discernible. Obviously many reasons could be advanced on anthropological, sociological and economical grounds: such reasons do no more than describe the changed conditions of human existence from different aspects without referring them to any higher principle. The cyclic theory of the Hindu doctrine, however, accounts for all these changes in a causal derivation. It implies a gradual 'falling away' from the Principle with the 'progress' of time or, more precisely, it implies a shift from the essential towards the substantial poles of manifestation.[22] The cause for this shift is inherent in manifestation itself and is, therefore, universal. It affects then simultaneously all the three domains of manifestation, the gross, the subtle and the formless; its effects are indefinitely extensive. From our point of view restricted to the present case it not only implies the gradual solidification of the world in the gross order,[23] the decline in sensitivity of the human mentality with respect to the subtle order, or the lessening of the accessibility of higher intellect (*Buddhi*)[24] in the formless order: it implies also the increase of anti-traditional, in a sense 'infernal' influences exerting themselves against the legitimate tradition.[25]

The application of this doctrine accounts for all the influences affecting the Hindu sacrifice and worship. With the 'progress' of time the human mentality became gradually duller and had to rely more and more upon symbolism as a support to grasp the nature of certain states unknowable by reason alone. The symbols themselves gradually solidified into stone; not only were they needed in ever-increasing quantity but had to become more personified, more explicit and detailed to facilitate their understanding. At the same time the sacrifice – which constitutes the symbolic act *par excellence* of every tradition – had to be more and more enclosed and walled in to protect it from the 'external' or internal influences and they became increasingly harmful with the passage of the times.[26]

The huge temple walled in by several enclosures is then not only the legitimate heir of the *Vedic* altar but, due to the causes inherent in the cyclic laws, its inevitable result. Once the situation is understood in this light one is no longer surprised about the enormous change that occurred in the external form of the original sacrificial altar. On the contrary, one would marvel that its essential content remained unchanged, that 'the "golden man", a schematic representation of man, which must be built into the altar' is still the basis of Hindu temple architecture after an elapse of more than 4,000 years.

3. SUBTLE FORMS OF THE INTERSPACE

The meaning and significance of the interspace between the outer wall and the innermost sanctum (Vimana) may be discernible from the several *Vastu Shastras* and *Shilpa Shastras* dealing with temple architecture. One must, however, not lose sight of the fact that these texts refer almost exclusively to the Vimana, which *is* the Hindu temple and treat the surrounding *Prakaras* and *Mandapams* very briefly, since they are simply an extension of the temple proper. It must be similarly borne in mind that the Hindu temple is not built for congregational worship but it is the house of the enshrined deity purely and simply. 'The *Puja* that is conducted inside (the sanctum) is both sacred and secret in character'.[27] However, the accessory structures, the *Mandapams* and enclosures are always circumambulated by the pilgrims who come to visit and to 'see' the enshrined god (*Darshana*) and serve as a space of transition between the external world and the Vimana proper. All this goes to show that the function of the interspace is not to be taken in the corporeal but rather in the mental sense insofar that by means of the symbolism inherent in their layout and by means of the great number of iconographic symbols housed under their roofs the 'elevation' of the mind from the gross to the formless order will be enhanced.

The Tantrasamuccaya, a treatise on temple architecture, refers to the construction of walls and interspace in the following stanza:

> The outer wall will be one-eighth of the breadth of the *Griha* (inner chamber), while the other (the inner wall) will be one-eighth of the breadth of the '*Garbha*'. All around in the interspace between the two (walls) (runs) the *Nadi*. In the case of an '*Alpagriha*' (small shrine) the two walls may be combined (into a single wall).[28]

The next stanza gives the following alternative for the *Alpagriha*:

> ... When the same (length and breadth) are divided by nine and (the inner wall) constructed as before, make a *Vithika* (or *Nadi* or interspace) and outer wall in the two rows (of quarters surrounding) beyond. And in the front quarter, at the outer row, construct a gateway.[29]

The Vimana of Lord Sundareswar seems to have been formed according to this last stanza, but our main concern here is not yet with the Vimana as a whole, but with the nature of the interspace to which these stanzas allude. It is said that in the interspace runs the *Nadi* which word denotes 'the luminous arteries of the subtle form'[30] of the human body, the seat of *Taijasa.* These luminous arteries must on no account be confused with the corporeal arteries, nor even with anything belonging to corporeal manifestation, since '*Taijasa*, the seat of which is in the dream state', '...and whose world is the domain of subtle manifestation'[31] is completely beyond any sensible qualities of the corporeal order. If, then, the inner sanctum is symbolic of the body of the sacrificial victim built into it schematically, the surrounding interspace, the *Vithika*, in which runs the *Nadi*, is symbolic of the subtle form of the body, or generally, of the subtle states of manifestation.

To return then to the overall layout of the Shri Minakshi Sundareswar from where these reflections arose, it can be concluded that the three enclosures which surround the two inner-sancta find their origin 'in the interspace between the two (walls)' where the *Nadi* runs. Once more, however, one must guard against a possible misunderstanding which would result in succumbing to a tempting fallacy, namely that the three enclosures are symbolic of three different orders of manifestation. It will be necessary to adopt here the relative point of view, alluded to before, as the basis of all symbolic interpretation.

The inner chamber (*Griha*) surrounded by an outer wall is the complete Hindu temple and any additional structure from the overall point of view is regarded as accessory and contingent. Now, if the interspace belonging to the Vimana corresponds symbolically to the subtle states of manifestation, it is obvious that it can mean neither more nor less if further accessory structures are built around it. Once, however, such a further enclosure or walling-in occurs, this accessory enclosure furnishes a relative point of view from where the whole of the Vimana will be regarded as the inner chamber (*Griha*), since it is not known – until so explored – that it contains an interspace already within itself. From this relatively external point of view the additional enclosure is taken then as the 'interspace' corresponding to subtle manifestation. Similarly, if an even further enclosure is built, from the point of view situated within the latter all that is beyond it is taken as the 'core' and the outermost enclosure corresponds again to subtle manifestation. As long as any of the inner enclosures are viewed from a point external to them, the actual *Griha* assimilates into itself all the enclosures that are located closer to the centre than the adopted point of view; and this assimilation holds good as long as the observer continues with his circumambulatory progress; in doing so he traces in fact the line of a spiral to which geometrical figure the successive circles of gradually decreasing radii can be likened on account of their continuous connection. The geometrical figures that correspond to the gross, subtle and formless states of manifestation 'are a straight line, a semicircle (or rather an element of the spiral) and a point'[32] and in this sense the circumambulatory spiral moves in fact in the subtle state until the 'point' at the centre is reached. The several enclosures (*Prakaram*)[33] surrounding the *Griha* then correspond in all cases to the order of subtle manifestation representing the several 'levels' or degrees inherent in the ideal state. This symbolism evolved on the horizontal section or the plan of the temple corresponds perfectly to the symbolism of the Gopuram, evolved on the vertical plane where the several tiers, or levels represented the successive degrees of subtle manifestation. There is, of course, no need to try to find exact correspondence between the numbers of tiers and of enclosures, since these numbers, varying as they are from case to case and temple to temple, must in no instance be taken literally; they symbolize simply the non-homogenous nature of the subtle state where manifestation occurs on several degrees, comparably in principle to the several degrees of manifestation occurring in the gross state.

In addition to all this the overall layout of the Shri Minakshi Sundareswar implies a symbolism of an even more general kind. The building of a temple, in the deepest sense, is the imitation of the process of creation, since 'every artistic operation, as such operation is envisaged by the tradition, is an imitation of what was done by the Gods in the beginning'.[34] The construction of the temple – as it will be shown more fully later – starts at the central 'point' and grows outwards, completing the quadrature from unity. It proceeds from the symbol of the formless order to the various degrees of the subtle order and establishes finally the 'connection', by means of the outermost walls and gates, with the gross 'world': just the same way as formless manifestation is the principle of formal manifestation and in turn the ideal is the principle of the sensible. The path of the devotee, however, reverses this order as he approaches from the outside towards the core; his progress is indicative of the inverse process of reintegration and reunification of which the goal is complete union (*Yoga*). Or, to use a different terminology, the act of construction is development whilst the act of circumambulation and approach is envelopment. The symbolism of the architectural layout is again perfectly explicit here, since during the process of spiral development none of the higher states – that is, inner enclosures – can be discovered, understood or experienced until the state immediately below it – that is, the enclosure external to it – has been assimilated and passed through.[35]

This involutory process implies another inverse analogy of a different kind, which exists between the manifested and unmanifested states of the being. In this sense it can be said that whatever is the least in the unmanifested is the largest in the manifested, or, again, whatever is the smallest in the manifested is the greatest in the unmanifested. The application of this analogy is clearly seen not only in the size of the Gopurams which decrease successively as they become more important, but also in the areas of the enclosures which diminish greatly as they become more sacred. In fact, the two smallest structures of the whole of the Shri Minaskhi Sundareswar, namely the two inner sancta, are the most important ones; in relation to the enormous extent of the total temple-area they are hardly more than a 'point'. It is then the dimensionless geometrical point, indeed the least of all corporeal manifestation, refers to the greatest of all principles governing manifestation, that is, to the unity of Principial Being.

4. THE PRIMORDIAL DUAD

The celebrated Hymn of Creation, known as the *Nasadiy Sukta* of the *Rig-Veda*

Pl. 1. Ganesha — stone sculpture in the Thousand Pillar Mandapam

Pl. 2a. South Gopuram, west face

Pl. 2b. South Gopuram, east face from inside the first enclosure

l. 2c. North Gopuram, west face

Pl. 3. West Gopuram, west face

Pl. 4a. West Gopuram, east face, upper stories

Pl. 4b. Sculptured details of the West Gopuram

Pl. 5. Barrel vault on the top of the West Gopuram

Pl. 6. Kirttimukha on the top of the West Gopuram of Sundareswar's Prakaram

Pl. 7a. Traders within the first enclosure of the Temple

Pl. 7b. Minakshi Nayaka Mandapam

relates the first differentiation of original Non-Duality in profoundly beautiful terms :

> Then there was neither Aught nor Naught,
> no air nor sky beyond.
> What covered all? Where rested all?
> In watery gulf profound?
> Nor death was then, nor deathlessness,
> nor change of night and day.
> That One breathed calmly, self sustained;
> naught else beyond It lay.
> Gloom hid in gloom existed first –
> one sea, eluding view.
> That One, a void in chaos wrapt,
> by inward fervour grew.[36]

'That One' who 'breathed calmly' 'in watery gulf profound' in the limitless, lightless, gloomy sea is the first differentiation of Brahma, of the absolutely unconditioned, undifferentiated and non-dual Supreme Identity; the first differentiation of all, 'the beginning of creation', is symbolized here by the difference between the primaeval, self-sustaining *breath* and the primordial *waters*, Universal Essence and Universal Substance. It is from their union, 'a void in chaos wrapt' that the first principle of manifestation, Itself unmanifest, the principle of Universal Being, 'That One...by inward fervour grew'.

The overall layout of the second enclosure of the Shri Minakshi Sundareswar refers to these principles with the astonishing clarity of its architectural composition. The second enclosure is roughly a square-shaped area embraced by a solid wall all round; but the area is divided or differentiated into two rectangles, one slightly larger comprising the Sundareswar temple, the other slightly smaller comprising the Shri Minakshi temple. This second rectangle is further divided into two areas : the *Pottamarai Kulam* (X) and the third enclosure of Shri Minakshi's Vimana. The relation of these parts establishes in architectural terms the constant preoccupation of Hindu symbolism with the two complementary principles of manifestation, since 'breath' and 'waters', *Purusha* and *Prakriti*, Essence and Substance, vertical and horizontal, male and female, Shiva-*Shakti*, Sundareswar and Minakshi, are simply different correlative terms denoting the one and the same thing. But before the full impact of this arrangement could be understood, the symbolic content of the Tank of the Golden Lilies needs further elucidation.

The *Veda* and the *Puranas* abound in references to the primaeval waters as the basis and support of all manifestation, as undetermined potentiality, as the all-sustainer of life. The relation of the 'waters' to the temple site is described specifically in the following passage of the *Tantrasamuccaya* :

> Let the revered Guru, for the purpose of installing the deity, fix a site in a sacred place, on the bank of a river, the shore of the sea, the place where rivers (or river and sea) meet, the

top and slope of mountains, in a forest, grove or garden, near the abode of the blest, in a village, capital, or city or in any other lovely place.[37]

The first four of these preferred places explicitly require the proximity of a natural expanse of water, the rest implicitly indicate the presence of ample moisture, since forest, gardens and communities cannot exist without it. In fact, there is no temple in India which would not be accompanied by a surface of water of same kind; if a natural water-course is absent, a large tank is dug from the earth. The spread of the water and the rising of the edifice are firmly bonded together. It is the same juxtapositioning of the 'horizontal' and the 'vertical' in a general sense which the elevation of the temple (Fig. 1) affirms from a special aspect. Reflecting and mirroring the soaring stone structure the water seems the natural counterpart of the edifice, its basis, origin and support. This substratum or substantiality is further expressed by 'the usual lotus-petal mouldings of architectural basements, (which seem to imply) that the whole building is supported by a widely extended lotus flower, that is to say, by earth and in the last analysis (on account of 'the lotus is the waters') by waters'.[38] From the general point of view the fundamental correlation of *Purusha* and *Prakriti* can then be expressed as 'temple' – 'waters', in which case the temple as a whole is the essential element supported by the waters, the substantial element.

There are, however, more specific points of view as well, from which the significance of the Tank of the Golden Lilies could be considered.

As the image of the sun reflected in water quivers and fluctuates in accordance with the undulations of the water, yet without affecting the other images reflected therein, so the modifications of one individual leave other individuals unaffected and, much more so, the Supreme Ruler Himself.[39]

Whereas the previously quoted hymn of the *Rig-Veda* X.129 dealt with the emergence of universal manifestation, this *Brahma Sutra* deals explicitly with the individual and therefore formal manifestation, more specifically with the individual make-up of man himself. 'It is the 'living soul' (*Jivatma*) which is here compared to the image of the sun in water as being the reflection (*Abhasa*) in the individual realm and relatively to each individual of the Light, principially one, of the 'Universal Spirit' (*Atma*); ...the water, therefore, can only represent here the potential sum of formal possibilities, or in other words, the realm of manifestation in the individual mode; and thus it leaves outside itself those formless possibilities, which, while corresponding with states of manifestation, must nonetheless be referred to the Universal'.[40]

In this sense the Hindu tradition differentiates between the possibilities of formless manifestation and the possibilities of formal manifestation, corresponding to the 'upper waters' and the 'lower waters' respectively. The 'upper waters' or 'celestial waters' are often compared to clouds (rain) and more explicitly to the sixteen mythological elephants, the offspring of *Airavata*, the first divine elephant. These eight pairs of male and female elephants became the supporters of the eight directions of space (*Dig-Gajas*), had wings and like clouds were free to roam about in the sky, until by a sudden misfortune some of them lost their wings and have been ever since forced to remain on the ground. 'And what is more, together with their faculty of roaming through the air, they forfeited also the divine power of assuming various forms at will'.[41]

It is remarkable how the Hindu thought can assimilate seemingly irreconcilable qualities in a given symbol. The elephant, the heaviest of all creatures, is assumed to fly and roam about freely in the sky! But is it not precisely through this frappant improbability that our attentions are immediately averted from the literal and directed to the symbolical? Now, the natural habits of the elephant are eminently connected to water; their shape vaguely resembles cumulus clouds; but what is more important, they are the strongest of all the animals and therefore the best 'supports' of the eight directional space which corresponds to formless manifestation. Their 'winged' or 'angelic' state signifies their freedom of local motion and their power to assume forms at will, like the clouds, place them above the limits of formal manifestation. They are thus verily the 'celestial waters' themselves, the symbol of the possibilities of formless manifestation, which, of course, include the possibilities of formal manifestation, as their 'wingless' or 'fallen' state in the terrestial elephant so succinctly indicates.

The Tank of the Golden Lilies, however, serves more tangible functions as well. The ritualistic bathing or submerging into the water is a daily repeated act of the orthodox Hindu which takes on especial significance at places of pilgrimage. The ritual *par excellence* of this aspect happens at the annual festival when the images of Shri Minakshi and Sundareswar are carried across the water and installed upon the small 'island' within the tank. By this 'walking on the waters', in other words by overcoming the undetermined potentiality, the creative act is presented anew: it was done by Krishna, the eighth *Avatar* (incarnation) of Vishnu when he jumped into the water-hole of the wicked serpent-king Kaliya, 'smote the water with his palms'[42] and eventually overcame the serpent by dancing on his head; it was done by Indra, the king of the *Vedic* gods, when he 'smote the serpent in his lair'[43] 'and is done by every solar hero and Messiah when he transfixes the Dragon and treads him underfoot'.[44]

Lastly, descending on to the plane of corporeal utility, the water tank serves not merely for washing away the sins of the religious, but also for washing off the dust and dirt of the day, thereby opening up the possibilities of the corporeal state which comes with the physical health and well-being in man.

All this goes to show that a symbol which is, at the same time, a physical fact can be looked upon not merely from different points of view, but also as representing concepts on several progressively higher levels of understanding. The *Pottamarai Kulam*, the Tank of the Golden Lilies, can be first looked upon as a corporeal possibility by keeping the bodies of the devotees clean; further, as an aesthetic possibility by delighting the visitor's mind; as a religious possibility by washing the sins of the pilgrims away; as a ritualistic possibility by being overcome in the representation of the creative act; as a symbol of possibilities of formal manifestation by reflecting the Supernal Sun as individual modifications; as a symbol of possibilities of formless manifestation by representing the celestial waters; and finally, as a symbol of *Prakriti*, the original polarization of Being, by being the 'support' of the temple, the total edifice and as such representing the totality of the possibilities of manifestation.

5. SYMBOLS OF UNIVERSAL POSSIBILITY

Possibility, conceived in an absolutely unlimited sense, has an even superior meaning to the foregoing 'which appears when it is carried over beyond Being Itself'.[45] Although this last and highest of all meanings can just the same way be symbolized by the waters – as it undoubtedly is by the unanswered question 'What covered all? Where rested all? In watery gulf profound?' – it will be more appropriate to return to the layout of the Shri Minakshi Sundareswar anew so that the Vimana of the Goddess is not left out of account.

Shiva's consort, Parvati, is the personified symbol of feminine substantiality in relation to masculine essentiality and stands, as an anthropomorphic image, for the same metaphysical concepts as the primordial waters stand in relation to primordial breath. An anthropomorphic image, however, lends itself to almost unlimited symbolic extension and differentiation in the verbal as well as in the iconographical mode: it can indicate theoretically indefinite number of aspects of attitudes which may be attributed to metaphysical principles from the relative point of view.[46] Thus from the Hindu worshipper's point of view, Parvati's prominence will vary according to the worshipper's inclination. For the Vaishnvites she will be no more than a minor goddess representing certain minor aspects of substantiality not contained in Lakshmi, Vishnu's consort; for the Shaivites her importance will greatly increase and most – if not all – aspects of substantiality will be identified with her; for the Shaktas she will achieve supreme importance – even exceeding that of Shiva's – and will be worshipped over and above the aspects of substantiality insofar as representing merely the possibilities of Being.

No useful purpose would be served here to examine in any detail the *Tantric* doctrine of *Shaktiworship*, which is – besides being highly complex and in the available renderings frequently obscure – the most secret of all doctrines operating in the Hindu tradition at present. One will be content to point out here anew that the Shri Minakshi Sundareswar temple is built on a sacred ground which, probably from time immemorial, but in any case for a long time, was regarded as such and supported several shrines and temples in succession; but what is even more significant, the temple is built to perpetuate the occasion when Shiva, as Sundareswar, married a maiden of the region who subsequently became known as Minakshi, the Fish-eyed Goddess (Pl. 17b). It is at the time of the marriage ceremony alone that the Hindu female takes precedence over the male and this is aptly shown by the bride taking the right side of the bridegroom.[47] This precedence, moreover, is expressed in the name of the temple, Shri Minakshi preceding Sundareswar. In all probability we are then faced here with 'Mother Earth' or with the 'Earth-Goddess' of untold antiquity, who, in the form of a local maiden, is 'revitalized' and 'fertilized' by her divine suitor. This act of marriage is perpetuated in the present instance and thus Shri Minakshi, reaffirming her connection with the waters in her 'fish-eyed' aspect, precedes in importance and significance Sundareswar, her Lord.

Assuredly, this is the highest of all possible meanings that one can attach to a symbol of substantiality and in this case it will not be sufficient to regard it simply as *Prakriti* constituting the substantial aspect of Universal Being. *Ishwara*, the Lord of created beings, the principle of manifestation unmanifest Itself, exalted a principle as He may be, is nevertheless qualified (*Saguna*) and the first limitation of the absolutely unqualified (*Nirguna*) Brahma. To assign then the highest of all possible meanings to substantiality in metaphysical terms, it will be necessary to regard it over and beyond Being Itself as 'Universal Possibility, conceived in an absolutely total manner, that is to say insofar as it embraces at the same time in Its Infinity the domains of manifestation and non-manifestation alike'.[48]

The temples of Shri Minakshi and of Sundareswar are placed side by side, fused into a coherent unity by their common Gopuram (U) and by the embracing wall approximating a square shape; they can be regarded as *Prakriti* and *Purusha*, constituting the substantial and essential aspect of and representing in their fusion the unity of Universal Being (*Ishwara*). But from a special point of view – which approaches the tendency of Shaktiworship – the Sundareswar shrine may be 'paired' with the water-symbol of the *Pottamarai Kulam* to represent Universal Being; the meaning of the Shri Minakshi temple is then carried over and beyond this last – and still limited concept – to represent Universal Possibility of being and non-being, manifestation and non-manifestation alike.

One can trace in the architectural layout the rather pronounced tendency of this last aspect without difficulty. The special situation of the Tiruvachi Gopuram already indicates the rather special importance which the temple beyond it should receive. Following the axial route from the East (Fig. 2), the door of the Shri Minakshi *Prakaram* is met 'sooner' than the Sundareswar *Prakaram*; but what is more important, the Vimana of Shri Minakshi is 'beyond' that of Sundareswar both from the aspect of the axial approach and of the enclosures, since the Vimana of Shri Minakshi is surrounded, in fact, by a total of four *Prakarams*. The temple of the Goddess, the Tank and the elephants, are all situated on the same side of the central axis of the total temple. From the eastern approach this appears to be the left, but in a heraldic sense it is the right side of the square, since the Goddess faces the east and Lord Sundareswar is thus on her left. Furthermore, if we reapply here the inverse analogy which exists between the physical sizes of the building and the metaphysical concepts it is called upon to represent, the precedence of Shri Minakshi over Sundareswar is again revealed, since here *Prakaram*, Vimana and *Griha* are all smaller than those of the corresponding case. The *Griha* of Shri Minakshi is in fact the smallest walled-in space of all and is therefore, at least from our latter points of view, the holiest shrine, verily the *sanctum sanctorum* of the entire temple.

NOTES AND REFERENCES

1. The terminology so far used in the first part of this study distinguishing simply between gross and non-gross states of manifestation – an inevitable point of view as long as the gross state has not been transgressed – needs proper extension here, since the passage from the outside to the inside of the temple has been symbolically accomplished.

   The Hindu metaphysics speaks of three worlds (*Tribhuvana, Triloka*) of manifestation, namely the gross or sensible order, the subtle or ideal order and the formless or principial order. The gross and the subtle orders belong to the individual realm, since they are both limited by form; the formless order, however, belongs to the Universal realm since it is no more limited by form. Cf. *Mandukya Upanishad, Shruti* 3-5, *Prashna Upanishad,* V.1-7, *Chhandogya Upanishad* I, 1.4.5, also René Guénon, *Man and His Becoming, op.cit.*, p. 87 ff.
2. 'The outer wall will be one-eighth of the breadth of the '*Griha*' while the other (the inner wall) will be one-eighth of the breadth of the '*Garbha*'. All around, in the interspace between the two (walls) (runs) the '*Nadi*' '. *Tantrasamuccaya, Patala* II, stanza 19.
3. One reason for the clockwise circumambulation is that the devotee presents always his *right* side towards the sanctum in this manner. It involves the macrocosmic and microcosmic meaning of right and left that we cannot consider here more fully.
4. The central or main entrance through the Raya Gopuram (A) leading axially to Shiva's shrine is actually right from the centre, whereas the *Ashta-Shakti Mandapam* (E) leading axially to Parvati's shrine is left from the centre. The right entrance is pronounced, the axis strongly developed, the left entrance is, so the speak, hidden, since it is not punctuated on the outside by a Gopuram and the axial approach is less strongly developed. All this relates very closely to the 'right' and 'left' way of approach to spirituality, the former coinciding with the masculine, essential pole, the latter with the feminine or substantial pole. The *Tantric* doctrine of the *Shakti worship* is highly secret and is practised not nearly as openly as Shiva-worship. The architectural arrangement seems to underline this distinction strongly. It is also remarkable that the Tiruvachi Gopuram (F) is placed actually in the 'interspace', that is into subtle manifestation.
5. J. Fergusson, *History of Indian and Eastern Architecture*, R.P. Spiers, London, 1891, p. 392.
6. The references for the foregoing description have been coordinated from the author's experiences gained during his visit to the temple in 1960; from Murray-Lothian, *Handbook for Travellers in India, Pakistan, Burma and Ceylon*, 1955; from *India: Photographs and Drawings* from the Office of Curator of Monuments, 1896; from Fergusson, *History of Indian and Eastern Architecture*, 1891; from Rowland, *The Architecture and Art of India*, 1953.
7. It has been observed before that the Tiruvachi Gopuram is not located actually on the line of the enclosing wall but it belongs there virtually.
8. It is not from the historical point of view that these reflections are undertaken here but rather to trace the development of symbolic communication, the immutable content of which is present in all its stages.
9. N.V. Mallaya, *Studies in Sanscrit Texts on Temple Architecture (with special reference to*

the Tantrasamuccaya), Annamalai University Publication, Annamalainagar, 1949, p. 100.

10. Titus Burckhardt, The Genesis of the Hindu Temple, *Etudes Traditionelles*, Oct.-Nov., 1953. A.B. Snodgrass' unpublished translation.
11. *Ibid.*
12. Obviously one must not think in terms of likeness of shape here: only the degenerated forms of art copy the external likeness of natural shapes. The preoccupations of sacred art are much more profound; it is the way, the manner in which nature evolves its forms that is analogically reproduced, as expressed also by the well-known Scholastic formula: *ars imitature naturam in sua operatione.*
13. N.V. Mallaya, *op.cit.*, p. 4.
14. *Ibid.*, p. 5.
15. From approx. 3000 B.C. to A.D. 1600.
16. A.K. Coomaraswamy, *History of Indian and Indonesian Art*, Goldston, London, 1927, p. 46.
17. Approx. A.D. 600. This distinction is borne out by the difference between the *Vedic* sacrifice, the *Yajna* and the present ritual offerings made to the image of the god, the Puja. See N.V. Mallaya, *op.cit.*, p. 105 ff.
18. *Ibid.*, p. 210.
19. One recalls here the much later wooden temples of Kerala in South India and more specifically those of Nepal which seem to have preserved, almost without modification, the timber post and beam layout and construction referred to in the Shastras.
20. Approx. the first few centuries A.D.
21. *Tantrasamuccaya*, *Patala* II, stanza 19, quoted previously.
22. See René Guénon, *The Reign of Quantity*.
23. For the solidification of the world see René Guénon, *The Reign of Quantity*, *op.cit.*, p. 146 ff.
24. In relation to man, the higher intellect (*Buddhi*) is not of a mental and therefore individual, but of a formless and therefore supra-individual order; it is the immediate, but transcendent principle of the individual state. Cf. René Guénon, *Man and His Becoming*, *op.cit.*, p. 65.
25. See René Guénon, *The Reign of Quantity*, *op.cit.*, under the successive stages of anti-traditional action, p. 229 ff.
26. 'In order that this symbolism may be fully understood in all its aspects, it is important to note that a wall acts both as a protection and a limitation: in a sense therefore it can be said to have both advantages and inconveniences; but insofar as its principal purpose is to ensure an adequate defence against attacks coming from below, the advantages are incomparably the more important, for it is on the whole more useful to anyone who happens to be enclosed within its perimeter to be kept out of reach of what is below, than it is, to be continually exposed to the ravages of the enemy, or worse still to a more or less complete destruction. In any case a walled space as such is not closed in at the top so that communication with superior domains is not prevented and this state of affairs is the normal one' (René Guénon, *The Reign of Quantity*, *op.cit.*, p. 216).

    It is interesting to note here that M. Guénon does not speak of architecture here, but uses the words and spatial symbolism inherent in architecture to describe a situation of a more general order. However, these words apply almost with perfect precision to the case of the walled-in Hindu temple. The communication with the superior domains will be developed in the last part of this study.

27. N.V. Mallaya, *op.cit.*, p. 210.
28. *Tantrasamuccaya, Patala* II, stanza 19, according to N.V. Mallaya, *op.cit.*, p. 47.
29. *Ibid.*, stanza 20.
30. René Guénon, *Man and His Becoming, op.cit.*, p. 96.
31. *Mandukya Upanishad, Shruti* 4. Cf. René Guénon, *Man and His Becoming, op.cit.*, p. 96, notes: 'In the text the subtle state is called Pravicta, literally 'predistinguished' because it is a state of distinction that precedes gross manifestation'.
32. René Guénon, *Man and His Becoming, op.cit.*, p. 118.
33. The *Tantrasamuccaya* describes five enclosures and their respective distances from the *Prasada*. See N.V. Mallaya, *op.cit., Patala* II, stanzas 73-77.
34. A.K. Coomaraswamy, *The Symbolism of the Dome, op.cit.*, pp. 12-13. This operation and its symbolism will be discussed in the third part of this study.
35. This coincides in any case with the normal spiritual progress. In exceptional cases the intermediate states are passed by, but are assimilated, nevertheless, virtually.
36. *Rig-Veda*, X.129, trans. Surendranath Dasgupta, *Indian Idealism*, p. 4. The same passage has been quoted in the first part of this study with reference to the *Makara* in a different translation.
37. N.V. Mallaya, *op.cit., Tantrasamuccaya, Patala* I, stanza 7.
38. Coomaraswamy, *Yakshas, op.cit.*, p. 57.
39. *Brahma-Sutras, Adhyaya* II, *Pada* 3, *Sutra* 53. According to René Guénon, *Man and His Becoming, op.cit.*, p. 55.
40. René Guénon, *Man and His Becoming, op.cit.*, pp. 55-56.
41. Matangalila I. The passage has been freely quoted from Zimmer, *Myth and Symbols, op.cit.*, p. 106.
42. *Vishnu Purana*, V. 7, according to Zimmer, *op.cit.*, p. 83.
43. *Rig-Veda*, VI.17.9, according to Coomaraswamy, *Symbolism of the Dome, op.cit.*, p. 21.
44. A.K. Coomaraswamy, *Symbolism of the Dome, op.cit.*, p. 20. Needless to say that in the quotations above the serpent and the dragon are equivalent symbols for the waters.
45. René Guénon, *Man and His Becoming, op.cit.*, p. 57.
46. Hence the many names and forms under which the Goddess is approached. Shiva's consort is known as Parvati, Durga, Kali, Uma, Minakshi etc. This differentiation or 'explicitness' even to the degree of appearing fastidious to a western mind, is a necessity inherent in the cyclic condition governing the present, to which reference has already been made with respect to the origin and evolution of the temple.
47. The same occasion is represented in the iconographical mode at the caves of Elephanta, where the sculptured group depicting the marriage of Parvati and Shiva shows Shiva to be on the left of Parvati. In all other normal cases when the couple is represented side by side the position is reversed.
48. René Guénon, *Man and His Becoming, op.cit.*, p. 57.

PART III

THE DIVINE MEASURE OF THE CORE

Prajna, the seat of which is in the state of deep sleep, is M, the third *Matra*, because it is the measure as well as because it is the end. He who knows this is in truth the measure of this whole and he becomes the final term.

Mandukya Upanishad
Shruti 11

1. VIMANA OF LORD SUNDARESWAR

Measure, understood in a qualitative sense, is equivalent to determination. By being measured, undetermined possibility becomes the support or 'ground' of existence, demarked and limited. According to the *Vishnu Purana*, Vishnu, in his incarnation of the Dwarf, measures with three steps the three worlds of manifestation, the gross, the subtle, the formless: by determining the limits and the 'extensions' of undetermined possibility. He creates the ground of universal existence. By being its 'measure', He becomes its determinant and its 'final term'.

Vimana, the term synonymous with *Prasada*, designating the inner temple proper, is composed of the root *Mana* (measure) and the prefix Vi (varied).[1] According to this definition Vimana must be understood as the synthesis of varied measures, varied not in a sense of being simply different for the sake of novelty, but varied because its determinants are of various orders. In the Vimana the most significant considerations of Hindu architecture crystallize: compared to it all the additional surrounding structures lose their significance. The *raison d'être* of the whole of the Shri Minakshi Sundareswar rests on the Vimanas or *Prasada*s of Shri Minakshi and of Sundareswar; in this structure is the symbol or image of the God installed within a small, dark space, the *Garbhagriha* (womb of germ), surrounded by thick walls (*Bhitti*) and crowned by the superstructure. The sacred character of this space is of such high degree that none but the officiating priests of the Brahmin caste are allowed to enter to perform the ritual offerings (Puja) to the Enshrined. The traditional writings dealing with the sacred science of architecture, the *Vastu-Shastras*, preoccupy themselves almost exclusively with the Vimana, which may or may not be surrounded by additional structures; but even if it were, as indeed it is in the case of the Shri Minakshi Sundareswar, the surrounding *Mandapams* and *Prakaras* deduct nothing from its importance. It is a temple *par excellence*, the synthesis of varied measures, the 'final term'.

The Vimana of Lord Sundareswar (Fig. 3), upon which all that follows is based, is not easily discernible and recognizable as a shape on its own (Pl. 18 left centre) since it is built in by the surrounding *Mandapam*. It is a small square chamber (*Griha* or *Garbhagriha*) constructed upon a base or socle (*Adhisthana*), surrounded by thick walls into which the pillars of the early temples coagulate. They form the leg (*Pada*) or pillar (*Stambha*) part of the structure; upon this rests the entablature (*Prastara*), emerging now visibly from the surrounding flat roofs (Pl. 19), which comprises the

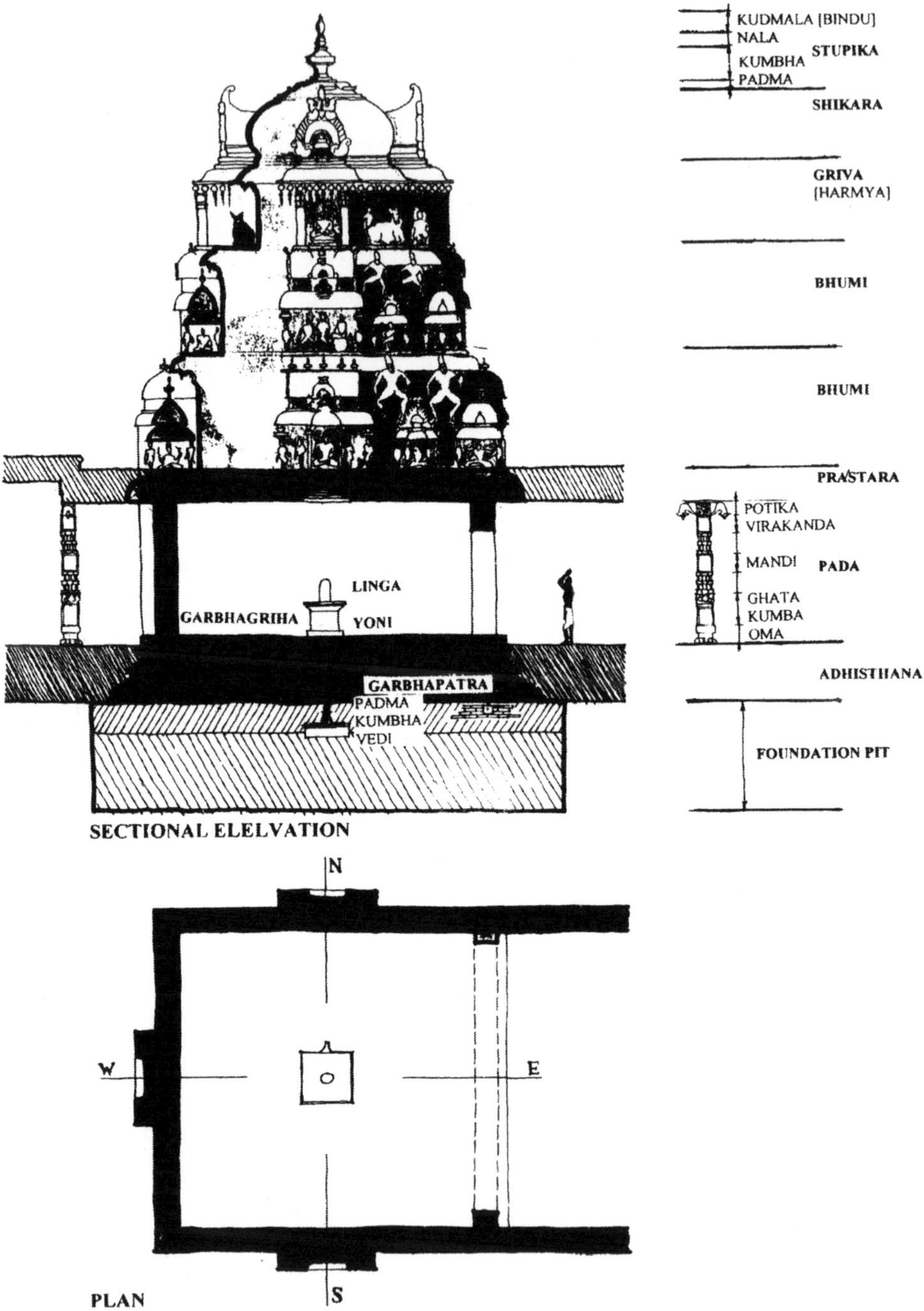

Fig. 3. Vimana of Sundareswar – sectional elevation

ceiling of the chamber, several further tiers or levels (*Bhumi*) in a truncated pyramidal form and the golden dome.

At the shoulder of this structure, where the pyramidal recession ceases, emerges the neck (*Griva*, *Gala*) covered by the dome-shaped head (*Shikhara*) which, in turn, is pierced by the axis of the finial (*Stupika*). The literary meaning of the term *Stupika* is 'top knot', 'tuft of hair' and comprises the distinctly separated shapes of the lotus (*Padma*), the pot (*Kumbha*), the lotus stalk (*Nala*) and the bud (*Kudmala*) or 'point' (*Bindu*).[2]

The external walls of the *Pada* and the surfaces of the *Prastara*, *Bhumi* and *Griva* are richly articulated architecturally and profusely covered with iconography. The inner walls of the womb, the *Garbhagriha*, however, are bare. The sole object within that dark space is the supreme symbol of Lord Sundareswar, the *Linga*; it is a short, polished, circular stone pillar rising from its square pedestal, the *Yoni*, placed directly under the vertical axis of the Vimana which emerges visibly in the finial.

As it appears now, the architectural arrangement of the Vimana of Lord Sundareswar consists of a small square chamber with a central vertical axis; it is solidly walled in, roofed by several tiers and eventually covered with a dome. Having reduced it to its essentials, one will forthwith begin to wonder in what way is the building of this structure conducive for the artist to 'contemplate divine ideas'[3] and why is the attached artistic operation 'an imitation of what was done by the Gods in the beginning'.[4] Alternatively, one could ask: 'In what respect is the 'fundamental diagram of the temple a symbol of the Divine Presence in the world?'[5] and 'In which sense is its ground 'the place for meeting and marriage of heaven and earth, where the whole world is present in terms of *measure* and is accessible to man.?'[6]

These questions give rise to concepts which, at first sight, transcend vastly the 'simple' form of the Vimana as described above and as found in almost every South-Indian village today. Is it not, rather, that the Vimana is nothing but an elaboration of four pillars roofed over with a stone slab which had no meaning, but only physical efficiency? Would one not have to guard rather carefully against the danger of reading symbolic meanings into simple physical 'facts'?. Is it not absurd to consider that the erection of a stone roof over an anthropomorphic image is 'an imitation of what was done by the Gods in the beginning'? To give a seriously considered answer to these latter questions is, however, just as difficult as to the former ones. One cannot sweep aside the possibility of profound considerations by the builders before having made a thorough study of all that has bearing upon the subject. Because 'a correct symbolic exegesis must be founded on a real knowledge of the principles involved and supported by cited texts, which are just as much facts as the monuments themselves'.[7] Clearly, the meaning of the Vimana is then not to be found by the examination of its external shape but rather by the comprehension of its inward form; a comprehension which will originate in the metaphysics of the doctrine and will be supported by the sacred texts, especially by the *Vastu-Shastras* pertaining to the art of architecture.

2. THE PRIMORDIAL SACRIFICE

Ishwara, the principal universal Being, is simultaneously the efficient and the material cause – or preferably, to use different expressions, the essential cause and the substantial cause — of manifestation. Prior to the act of creation, which follows every dissolution according to the Hindu theory of cycles, it is in the unmanifested state of universal Being 'that the different objects of manifestation, including those of individual manifestation, external as well as internal,... subsist in a principal mode';[8] all separateness inherent in existence ceases, being unified 'non-distinctively' in Being. This state is the sum of the qualities of pure Being (*Sat*), Consciousness (*Chit*) and Beatitude (*Ananda*), generally united as *Sachchidananda* and it is by this latter term that the divine state of the Lord is qualified (*Saguna*). Blissful and exalted as this state might be in itself, from the contingent, the human point of view it is not without disadvantages. The world is at standstill, strictly speaking it is non-existent. The countless possibilities of the manifested worlds (*Samsara*) rest absorbed in 'Primordial nature' (*Mula-Prakriti*). The play of manifestation (*Lila*) has not yet begun anew, separate existence in the individual mode is impossible and human life with its incalculable variety of joy and pain, but also with its possibility of spiritual progress, is denied. From this relative, human point of view the undifferentiated state of Being can easily be looked upon as frighteningly selfish in character.

The metaphysical 'act' of manifestation, which consists on the one hand in the separation of *Purusha* and *Prakriti* emerging from their undifferentiated state and, on the other hand, the 'victorious' action of Essence over the 'self-preserving reluctance' of Substance, is told in countless myths of the *Vedas* and of *Puranas*. The emergence of manifested existence is recounted time and again as the primordial fight between the *Devas* (gods) and the *Asuras* (demons) in which the *Asuras* are overcome; the selfish dragon retaining the life giving waters of the universe is transfixed by Indra when he 'smote the serpent in his lair'[9] and much the same way by Soma when he 'fixed the miser'.[10] The solar heroes, Indra, Soma, or generally the *Devas*, are man's friends. The dragons and serpents his foes; their fight occurs, however, solely from the human point of view, because the deadly enemies are in concord behind the scenes, since in reality they are One. The dismembering, transfixing and overcoming are then solely the outward aspect of an inward act which is, performed within the blissful unity or to use different words, within the sacred state of Being. It is then a sacred act (cf. Latin *sacrafacere*), a sacrifice *in divinis*, resulting in the disintegration of Unity to give room to multiplicity in the manifested worlds; and it is this disintegrated imperfection which has to be reintegrated into Perfection in the sacrifice, performed now in turn by man, because 'Once heaven and earth were united, separating, they said: Let what is suitable to the sacrifice be common to both?'.[11]

The primordial sacrifice is alluded to also in the myth of the titan king Tvastri, whose one cup is made into four by the three Ribhus. These 'men of the interspace or air' are said to have quartered the titan's cup 'as it were, measuring out a field'.[12] By this quartering and by 'measuring out a field', the three 'powers' create Three

Worlds (*Triloka*) and thus proceed from unity to quadrature. A similar function is attributed in many instances to the Sun, often described as the titan's eye, in that he surveys, experiences and 'feeds upon' the worlds and 'measures out the chthonic regions'.[13] Here again the same procedure is implied: the undifferentiated unity of the apparent circular path of the Sun reflects itself as fourfold upon the earth in the four solar stations 'representing the limits of the solar motion in the four directions (motion daily from East to West and back again and annually from South to North and back again)'.[14] In this way the four cardinal directions are the result of the heavenly circle and this four-quartered-ness or four-sided-ness, gives 'measure' to the earthly plane represented by the square. Furthermore, the actions of the three Ribhus can also be understood in the spatial sense as 'measuring out' a dimensionless 'field' by determining its limiting conditions and creating the three dimensions of space. This operation is indispensable to the extension of any horizontal plane in terms of the four quarters 'and it is in this sense that we proceed from unity in quadrature by means of a triangle'.[15] In planar geometry this is the operation which results in a square from the circle, as it will be seen later on; in solid geometry it is expressed by a four-sided pyramid resting over a square base.

The sacrifice *in divinis*, that is the creation of the manifested worlds, is then a departure, a *fall* from principal Unity and thus analogous to *development* from Unity to quadrature, or more generally, multiplicity. The sacrifice performed by man, however, must reverse this process and will become analogous to envelopment from multiplicity to Unity. This dual procedure, which at the same time is the origin *and* the aim of individual existence, finds its expression in sacred architecture almost by necessity: the act of construction corresponds to creative development, the meaning of the completed form as a symbol – to envelopment, that is to spiritual envelopment as experienced and *seen* from the human point of view (*Darshana*). Precisely in this sense will the Vimana be shown to represent in its construction the act of creation and in its symbolic meaning if such an expression is permitted – the act of reintegration.

3. THE VASTUPURUSHA MANDALA

According to the many myths of Hindu tradition the fall from unified Being (*Sattva*) into separate existence (*Bhuta*) has something frightening, *asuric* and undetermined in its nature. 'Once there was some existing thing not defined by name, unknown in its proper form in blocked heaven and earth; seeing that the *Devas* (gods) seized it of a sudden and laid it on the earth face downwards. In the same position as they were when they seized it, the *Devas* stayed on it where it lay. Brahma made it full of gods and called it *VastuPurusha*'.[16] This fallen existence, unprincipled and chaotic as it appears in its primordial fall, needs to be seized upon and fixed by principles and orders. The manifested world must operate according to law; the origin of this law is in the Divine Essence whose emissaries are the *Devas*. Only after this can 'the existing thing undefined by name, unknown in its proper form' receive its name, *Vastupurusha* and its proper form, the square. 'The symbol of its ordered extensiveness is the square so that it is even said of him: long ago there was a demon in the shape of a square'.[17] 'The head of the *Vastupurusha* lies in the East, in the site of 64 squares'.[18] It lies face down on the earth or even within the earth. It is sometimes spoken of as the supporter of the earth, sometimes as the Lord of the maiden Earth, who is inseminated by him. But whatever his aspect, 'once laid on the ground, is measured out in squares, from east to west with the course of the sun, from light to darkness. He is one and uniform; all the possibilities of existence are displayed in the tranquillity of his recumbent state'.[19]

Over his schematic figure the Hindu temple is built from the *Vedic* times up to the present day. The full name of the figure, as a rule, is *Vastupurusha-Mandala.* The first term is derived from *Vastu* (existence) which with accent, *Vastu*, denotes dwelling places and planned sites. The second term, *Purusha*, means 'Person', especially 'Divine Personality', 'Essence' and in its highest aspect 'Divine Impersonality' (*Uttama Purusha*). In the present context *Purusha* is regarded as the efficient cause of existence (*Vastu*, *Bhuta*) in the first place, but also as a determinant and 'measure' of undefined existence in the form of order in the second place. In this form he takes up his residence (*Vastu*) on the earth. The third term, *Mandala*, denotes a geometric figure which is a closed polygon; the form of the polygon of *Vastupurusha* is a square, which is the expression of the celestial rule over the earthly substance. The *Vastupurusha-Mandala* is therefore the image of the Divine Personality as it resides, in His immanent aspect, in manifested existence.

The foregoing discussion aimed to expose, perhaps in a somewhat lengthy way, certain fundamental concepts and their relationships which constitute the basis of all the operations attached to the construction of the Hindu temple. It aimed to show, on the one hand, that manifested existence is the result of the primordial sacrifice of undifferentiated Unity and that this 'fall' from the Principle is demonic and *asuric* in nature until it becomes determined and receives its 'measure'. On the other hand, the cited texts intended to establish that the procedure from Unity to quadrature is analogous to the 'measuring out of a field' because it is in the four-quartered square that the undivided heavenly circle is expressed on the earthly plane of existence. All this is perfectly synthesized in the *Vastupurusha-Mandala* which expresses by its name (*Nama*) the sacrificial descent of the Divine Personality into His earthly residence and by its square form (*Rupa*) the measure and determination which existence receives through the reflection of the heavenly rule.

The *Vastupurusha-Mandala* is then verily the 'marriage of heaven and earth' in a sacrifice 'common to both'. It is laid out upon the sacred ground which will support the Vimana, the 'synthesis of varied measures'.

4. FROM UNITY TO QUADRATURE

He who is disposed to duties with reference to castes and stages of life, who is enriched with wealth which is the outcome of the observance of the rules prescribed thereon, whose mind tends towards the installation of an image for the performance of daily worship of the Supreme Person, must first seek a distinguished 'Guru'.

Pl. 7c. Gopurams to the Minakshi and Sundareswar Prakaram (west)

Pl. 7d. The western gateway, looking east

Pl. 8a. Saraswati — stone sculpture in the Thousand Pillar Mandapam

l. 8b. Gate of the Sundara Pandya Gopuram

Pl. 9. Nandi Mandapam with the sacrificial post in front of the Prakaram of Sundareswar

Pl. 10. Nandi — stone sculpture in front of the Prakaram of Sundareswar

Pl. 11. Nateshwarh — the Dancing Shiva — stone sculpture in front of the Prakaram of Sundareswar

Pl. 12a. Yali — from the row of pillars in front of the Minakshi Prakaram

Pl. 12c. Mandapam in front of the Minakshi Prakaram

Pl. 12b. Mandapam in front of the Minakshi Prakaram

Pl. 13. South Indian Pillar with lotus bud capital at the Tank of the Golden Lilies

Let this 'Guru' be a priest, a man of high birth, one sanctified by the observance of a host of purificatory rites, a knower of the essence of the '*Vedas*' and the '*Agamas*' learnt in proper manner, a follower of the traditions bearing on the system of caste and the stages of life, one consecrated to religious observances, one who is skilful and has practised '*Tapas*' and who is a believer in the existence of God.

Now, the venerable *Acarya* (Guru), selected by one desirous of doing religious duties, should, together with the *Murtipas* (disciples) carry out in order the work promised, beginning with *Bhuparigraha* (selection of site) and ending with *Tirthabhiseka* (bathing the image in connection with the installation ceremony).[20]

With these stanzas the author of the *Tantrasamuccaya* inaugurates the building of a new temple. The real builder is the patron (*Yajamana*, lit. the sacrificer) on whose behalf the temple is built; he must select a spiritual preceptor (Guru or *Acarya*) who is the director of all operations in the doctrinal and metaphysical sense. The Guru is the spiritual authority upon whom all temporal operations depend: he selects the suitable site and performs the rites, notably the ones which mark the beginning and the end of the construction. All this goes to show that the building of a Hindu temple has never become a profane operation set with all too frequently in other parts of the world. The authority of the traditions has been preserved continuously in India and consequently building is just as much a metaphysical rite as it is a physical skill. The essential layout and arrangement, however, belong to the sacred Tradition: it is simply the skill of the execution that belongs to the artist.[21] Clearly then it is impossible to talk about a profanization, a humanization, or a 'Renaissance' in Hindu architecture. The presence of the Guru is the guarantee that the whole process of temple-building is just as sacred in character today as it was in *Vedic* times. In fact, the metaphysical significance of the *Vedic* altar has been preserved to such an extent, that one can say without exaggeration that the *Vedic* altar is the pristine prototype of the present Vimana.[22]

The actual building operations connected to the Vimana are carried out by the *Shilpins* (trained artists or craftsmen) of whom there are four kinds enumerated by all the *Vastu-Shastras*: *Sthapati* (the architect, master-builder), *Sutragrahi* (the surveyor-draftsman), *Vardhaki* (builder-painter), *Taksaka* (carver, i.e. sculptor-carpenter). 'Without these four nothing can be undertaken. Therefore all these four, the *Sthapati* and others, should always be honoured'.[23]

These craftsmen are traditional in the strictest sense of the word; they were born in castes which carried on the craft for untold number of years. Foremost of them is the *Sthapati* who is not merely an artist but 'plays often a priestly role while offerings are being made to the various deities presiding over the quarters'.[24] He is said to claim equal standing with high-caste Brahmins, even 'certain sacerdotal privileges'.[25] To some extent he seems to receive and transmit to the constructional operations the spiritual authority which resides in the first place with the Guru. In other words, what the Guru is in relation to all matters connected with temple-building from conception to consecration, the *Sthapati* is in relation to its period of construction.

There is something analogous here in the case of the *Sthapati* and his three craftsmen to the myth of *Tvastri* and his three *Ribhus* and to *the Brahmana* and his three ritual priests of the sacrifice. The fundamental procedure from Unity to quadrature is once again encountered in the sense that the 'unborn form' of the Vimana, residing in the *Sthapati's* mind in a principal mode, becomes actual through the fourfold operation of the *Sthapati*, the *Sutragrahi*, the *Vardakhi* and the *Taksaka.* It is hardly surprising then that their first operation, which is symbolically as well as constructionally the most important one in the erection of the temple, presents the procedure from Unity to quadrature in concrete geometrical terms (Fig. 4).

Having levelled the ground which is at the north or south of the Equator, erect a gnomon (1) of twelve angulas in height. With three points marked at the end of shadows projected at different times as the centre (2, 3, 4), describe three circles (of equal radius) and thus produce two (figures which resemble) fishes (5, 6). Then extend lengthwise two threads starting from the Susumnashiras (Madhyanadi, i.e. central chord) of the two fishes till they meet at a certain point (7). From here till the central point at the base of the gnomon lay a thread and thus determine the southern and northern quarters (8); and then from this (line) fix the rest (eastern and western quarters)?[26]

The text of the Manasara is more explicit regarding 'the rest', that is the eastern and western quarters. Accordingly, a circle is drawn with radius (1-7) from the base of the gnomon and two more circles from centres 7 and 8 with a somewhat larger radius than before. The intersection of these two circles produces a third fish whose head and tail points determine the east-west line (9-10). The intersections of four more circles drawn from centres 7, 8, 9, 10 mark the four points of intermediate directions (11, 12, 13, 14) which are at the same time the corners of the basic square, the *Vastupurusha-Mandala.*

This geometric construction, carefully[27] reproduced from the texts, crystallizes in itself all the symbolism alluded to before. The point at which the gnomon is erected represents the undifferentiated Unity, the 'origo' of the whole construction, the Source of manifestation. The vertical gnomon in relation to the horizontal plane corresponds to the relation of essence to substance[28] and, in fact, it is the changeless action of the stationary vertical which imprints itself in the form of a moving shadow upon the receptive horizontal plane. The horizontal plane is the ground, upon which the 'act' of the vertical manifests itself; in the absence of the plane such a manifestation would be impossible since the shadow could not be traced. The vertical gnomon and the horizontal plane correspond then to the first separation of *Purusha* and *Prakriti* from the undifferentiated 'Point' which is common to both.

From another point of view the shadow of the gnomon is caused by the apparent path of the sun as it projects itself upon the earth. And apparent we say assuredly, since it is the earth which moves under the motionless sun just as *Prakriti's* actionless change relates to the changeless action of *Purusha.* By means of the gnomon, which is akin in nature to It, the 'Titan's eye' descends upon the earth in the image of the *fallen*[29] shadow. Moreover, the selected three points (2, 3, 4) with the *unique* point at the base of the gnomon (1) correspond to the several

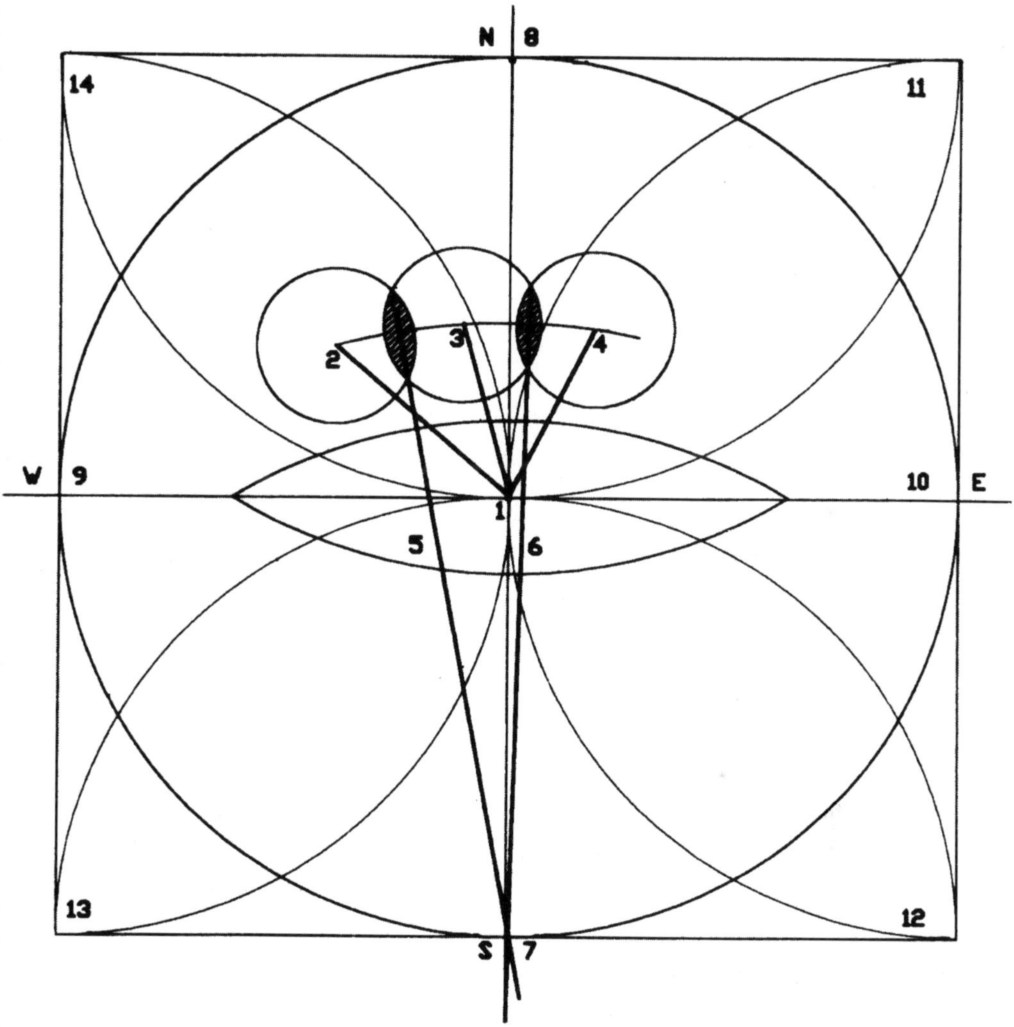

Fig. 4. Orientation of the *Vastupurusha-Mandala* on a site north of the Equator, according to the *Tantrasamuccaya*

quarternaries referred to before whose, joint 'operation' performs the work. Through the three points of the shadow is the first direction found with respect to the origin (7-1) and through three other circles (drawn from centres, 1, 7 and 8) the second direction, which together with the first, marks the four cardinal points (7, 8, 9, 10). In this way the passage from Unity to quadrature by means of ternary is accomplished; by means of four more circles finally the square is produced. The east-west and north-south lines, intersecting at the base of the gnomon, mark the cross which determines the four quarters of the square and the four cardinal points; these, together with the four corners of the square, represent the eight directions of space (7, 8, 9, 10, 11, 12, 13, 14) as imprinted upon the level of the earth. The previously undefined plane 'unknown in its proper form' has now been 'measured' by the Sun (*Purusha*), who descending upon earthly existence (*Vastu*) has taken up his residence (*Vastu*) in it. The one cup of the Titan Svastri has now been quartered and from the heavenly circle the earthly square achieved.

Yet from another point of view the initial operation of the four Shilpins reveals a further symbolism of utmost importance. The east-west and north-south lines intersecting at the base of the gnomon together with the vertical axis of the gnomon now thought of as penetrating also below the surface of the ground, form a three-dimensional cross; they establish the three (or six) dimensions of space originating at the common 'point'. The operation of the three Ribhus or 'powers' analogous to the three dimensions is indispensable for the extension of any horizontal plane or 'ground of existence' measured in terms of the four cardinal directions. The vertical axis, which coincides with the vertical axis of the Vimana and, further, with the 'Axis of the Universe' is the source of any plane of existence, be it in the gross, subtle, or formless order. This symbolism will be developed more fully in the last part of this study: the three-dimensional cross, however, appears at the very beginning of the construction of the Vimana and this shows its profound significance. It determines the square diagram of horizontal existence, which is the *Vastupurusha-Mandala*. Within, exhausted from his sacrifice and from his fall, lies prostrate its Lord, his head in the east, facing his Earthly Bride who receives His seed.

5. PEGGING AND INSEMINATING THE GROUND

The *Vastupurusha-Mandala* is yet the ideal state of pure geometry.[30] It needs to be seized and fixed. The Devas, seeing it 'seized it of a sudden' and when they seized it, they 'stayed on it where it lay'. The bond between the ideal and the sensible form needs to be established as directed by the next stanza of the *Tantrasamuccaya*:

> Let the master facing the east and chanting '*Astramantras*' on pegs which are firm and made of the tree called '*Punna*' and measuring one '*Hasta*' in height and one-fourth '*Hasta*' in circumference, plant one peg at the centre of the plot first and the rest round the boundary line of the chosen temple site in the (eight) quarters terminating with the Ishana (north-east) quarter; let him then twine a cord round each of the pegs twice and thus encircle that whole boundary in proper order: thus let him choose a plot for every God.[31]

The pegging of the boundary is, of course, a perfectly logical and necessary operation from the strictly constructional point of view. But an operation which works as a physical necessity in the gross order does not lose its symbolic significance with respect to other orders of manifestation: on the contrary, it becomes eminently suitable to such extensions, since, as pointed out before, a true symbol in a sense *is* what it symbolizes. The essential distinction between the profane and the symbolic point of view is simply this: that a profane operation preoccupies itself merely with the appearances of the sensible order, whilst the symbolic operation transposes these appearances into the ideal and causal orders, since it is from these higher principles that the sensible manifestation derives its existence. Every traditional artist uses the operations of his craft as a support to 'contemplate divine ideas', that is, to understand the principles governing gross manifestation. Identifying himself with and losing himself in his artistic operation he treads the path of spiritual progress.

In the operation of the pegging, besides the obvious analogy between the Devas and the nine pegs, there is a profound aspect to be discerned. In the Shaivite tradition *Vastupurusha* is *Vastopati-Ishana*, that is Shiva sunk into the ground. He is also referred to as *Vastu-Deva* who dwells in the nether worlds and is the upholder of the earth. The *Vastu-Deva* is *Vastu-Naga* (serpent), the support of all architecture, worshipped as a golden serpent.[32] 'The serpent underground, an Endless Residium (*Ananta, Shesa*) is the non-proceeding godhead, Death, overcome by the proceeding Energy with whom the Axis of the Universe, its exemplary support, is identified...'.[33] 'The astrologer shows what spot in the foundation is exactly above the head of the snake that supports the world. The mason...drives the peg into the ground at this particular spot in such a way as to peg the head of the snake securely down...if this snake should ever shake the world to pieces'.[34] 'The Gods said, 'Come, let us make steady this support'.[35] 'All above a polished shaft, all a piercing spike below. Where they marked the Naga's head deep the point was driven down'.[36]

These citations rejoin and shed a new light upon the 'smiting of the serpent' alluded to before. But whilst the solar hero's victory over the selfish dragon opened up the possibility of universal manifestation, the immediate result of his victory is frightening, *asuric* and unsecure considered from the plane of formal manifestation. The result of the 'fall', the possibility of formal manifestation in its undefined and unintelligible state, is 'infernal' as long as it is not acted upon by the Intelligible Light which determines its undefined extent and renders it 'steady' lest it 'should ever shake the world to pieces'. The peg is the penetrating essence into the receptive substance, the fixed point around which formal manifestation will expand in a foreseeable and measured way determined by the directions of the horizontal cross. In other words, the primordial serpent transfixed by the solar hero reappears on a lower plane as the *Naga* within the earth, to be transfixed anew by the solar hero's counterpart. Moreover, the quartered state of principal Unity which is the formal expression of the 'fall' and which is a necessity from the relative point of view of formal manifestation, is, nevertheless, an awesome sacrifice from the principal point of view; its split state must be reunited without delay by referring it back to the

Principle, which is accomplished by encircling the peripheral pegs with the cord and tying them firmly to the centre. This threading of the circle is properly speaking the miraculous feat achieved by another solar hero, the Bodhisattva Jotipala, a superlative marksman. Standing in the centre of a four-cornered field 'his arrow, to which a scarlet thread has been attached, penetrates in succession four marks placed at the four corners of the arena, returning through the first of these marks to his hand, thus describing a circle which proceeds and ends in himself as its centre'.[37]

These quotations refer to the profound principles conditioning manifested existence. The theme could be amplified with many further references drawn from widely differing sources resulting in a development to which there would be practically no end. Yet the interpretation moving on a rational plane must perforce remain obscure, since the symbolic content was never meant to be understood in a logical mode. As it has been indicated before, the whole *raison d'être* of symbolic communication is aimed to transcend the rational mind and to pave the access to the supra-rational faculty, the 'higher intellect' (*Buddhi*). In fact, a rational interpretation of a symbol might close just as many vistas as it might open and one could add that the meaning which remains hidden is probably the more significant one.

Traditional symbolism will therefore elucidate by indefinitely varied means what at a cursory glance might appear the 'same thing'. The several and often contradictory aspects, however, are purposefully chosen to invalidate an over simplification made in the formal or logical manner and to warn the seeker of the truth that the real meaning will perforce stay hidden until certain mental barriers are not left behind. In this connection one may remark that the worship of the *Vastu-Naga* in the form of a golden (solar) serpent is logically irreconcilable with the sacrilegious and 'brutal' act of pegging its head; this shows only too clearly that the supra-formal states of manifestation will not reveal their 'nature' or meaning in the rational mode.

The *Vastupurusha-Mandala*, secured by the pegs and related to the centre, is not the actual plan of the Vimana, nor of the whole site. It is the sacred diagram (*Yantra*) which signifies the ideal state in the sense as the sensible presupposes the ideal. The *Mandala* rules and directs the gross form of the temple which can never correspond exactly to the ruling subtle form.

The square of the *Mandala* is divided into 8 x 8 = 64 (or 9 x 9 = 81) minor squares, which are regarded as forming two separate borders around the centre, presided over by various deities (Fig. 5). The central plot is assigned to Brahma who is identified with the Spiritual Centre. Surrounding Him are placed the twelve deities of the ruling stars, forming the first border. In the outer border are located the thirty-two *Vedic* gods, of which Surya (Sun) in the East, Soma (Moon) in the North, Varuna (Waters) in the West and Yama (Death) in the South, rule over the plots corresponding to the cardinal directions. Outside the square four demons and four demonesses reign over the eight cardinal directions. Their total number is 8 + 32 + 12 = 52 + 1 = 53 and their significance is to coordinate into one ideal

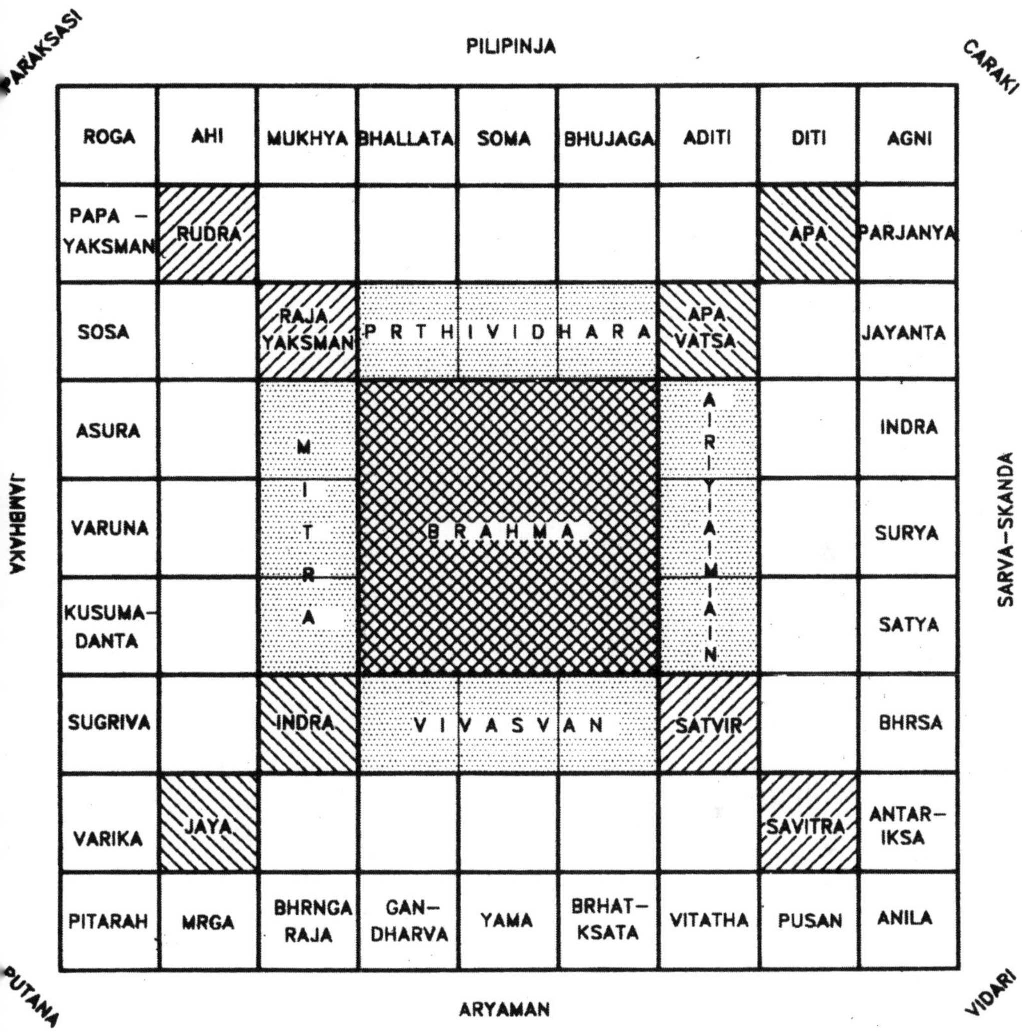

Fig. 5. The Vastupurusha-Mandala

state the, relationship of space and time based on complex astrological considerations. The number of days in a month (32), the number of months (12) and the number of weeks (52) in a year, the motion of the sun, the moon and the planets, the effect of the Ecliptic are all fused into coherent unity. The heavenly rule, expressed through the medium of time reigns in the form of the Devas over the body of the *Vastupurusha*, over the three dimensions of space and over the eight directions of the horizontal plane.[38] 'In the same position as they were when they seized it, the Devas stayed on it where it lay'.

The rituals that follow are all meant to purify, inseminate and prepare the earth to bear the Vimana. A foundation pit is dug to the height of a man standing with outstretched arms. After purification the earth is filled in again and consolidated so as to leave a quarter of the height unfilled (Fig. 3). An altar (*Vedi*) is erected then within the pit and sacrificial offerings are made to *Vastu* (*Vastu-puja*) who rules over the construction. The laying of the foundation stone (*Adharashila*) follows next, 'which will have a low space in the centre which will be filled with grains. Over the seat of grains will be placed, according to the rites, the *Nidhikalasha*, the sacred pot' (*Kumbha*).[39] It contains precious stones and metals and the goddess *Shakti* is invoked therein. 'On the jar a stone lotus (*Padma*) is placed, on the stone lotus a stone tortoise, on the stone tortoise a silver lotus and on it a silver tortoise, on the silver tortoise a gold lotus and on it a gold tortoise. From there a funnel-shaped tube, the *Yoganala*, made of copper, leads up to the plinth (*Yanman*)'.[40] In this rite the lotus represents the *Shakti*, or more specifically Lakshmi, the tortoise an incarnation of Vishnu, her consort. Their successive pairing in stone, silver and gold refers to the potential development of the three worlds: the gross (earth), the subtle (air) and the formless (heaven). Lotus and tortoise, Lakshmi and Vishnu, substance and essence, understood on their appropriate levels as complementary principles, are the source of manifestation of all the worlds. The possibility of their successive enfoldment is directed into the visible temple from below by the funnel-shaped tube, the *Yoganala*.

Only after this ritual are the first bricks made and laid out, according to the rite, so as to form square with a pit in its centre.[41] Once more the Guru invokes the goddess *Shakti* as creative energy and lowers into the pit, on an auspicious day, the *Garbhapatra*, a copper casket made in a cubical form, containing precious stones, herbs and roots. The *Garbhapatra* is the source of universal production. It is the womb (*Garbha*) and contains the seed in its triple form (*Bindu*, *Nada*, *Bija*) that is essentiality understood on the causal, ideal and sensible level.[42]

Mother Earth, the supporter and preserver of all things, is addressed now in the most endearing terms to shelter the seed and to bring forth the Person (*Purusha*), the new 'golden man' of the temple (*Prasada*).

After this important ceremony, the *Garbhavinyasa*, the foundation pit is filled in. The preparations are concluded. The earth, the horizontal plane of existence, has received its measure, its extension and development are complete; the limits are determined, the boundaries drawn. The all-supporting, tenebrous serpent has been pegged to stay steady. *Vastupurusha*, who has descended from the sky and been fixed into position, inseminated the Earth and from his own seed he will be reborn in the form of the Golden *Purusha* whose body is the Vimana. He will be built into the temple facing the sky and through his sacrifice all that has been quartered will be *One* once more.

NOTES AND REFERENCES

1. Cf. N.V. Mallaya, *op.cit.*, p. 275.
2. According to all the traditional writings constituting the *Vastu-Shastra*, for example the *Tantrasamuccaya*, the *Manasara*, *Shilparatna*, etc., the vertical divisions of the Vimana are invariably sixfold: socle (*Adhisthana*), leg (*Pada*), entablature (*Prastara*), neck (*Griva*), head (*Shikhara*) and top knot (*Stupika*). The *Tantrasamuccaya* gives the fixed proportions of heights as 1:2:1:1:2:1 respectively, but these proportions may vary, as they do, according to other authorities. The actual proportions of the Shri Minakshi Sundareswar are not discernible from photographs, but it is evident that the superstructure, comprising the last four terms, is greatly elaborated and heightened.
3. N.V. Mallaya, *op.cit.*, p. 3.
4. A.K. Coomaraswamy, *Symbolism of the Dome*, *op.cit.*, pp. 12, 13.
5. Titus Burckhardt, *The Genesis of the Hindu Temple*, *op.cit.*, p. 6.
6. Stella Kramrisch, *The Hindu Temple*, *op.cit.*, p. 7. The italics are mine.
7. A.K. Coomaraswamy, *Symbolism of the Dome*, *op.cit.*, p. 22.
8. René Guénon, *Man and His Becoming*, *op.cit.*, p. 105.
9. *Rig-Veda*, VI.44.22, according to Coomaraswamy, *Symbolism of the Dome*, *op.cit.*, p. 21.
10. *Rig-Veda*, VI.17.9, according to Coomaraswamy, *Symbolism of the Dome*, *op.cit.*, p. 21.
11. *Taittiriya Brahmana* I.1.3.2-3, according to Stella Kramrisch, *op.cit.*, p. 7 n.
12. *Rig-Veda* I, 110.3-5, according to A.K. Coomaraswamy, *Symbolism of the Dome*, *op.cit.*, p. 2.
13. *Rig-Veda*, V.81.3; V.85.5. *Ibid.*, p. 3.
14. A.K. Coomaraswamy, *Symbolism of the Dome*, *op.cit.*, p. 6.
15. *Ibid.*
16. *Brihat Samhita*, LII, 2-3, according to Stella Kramrisch, *The Hindu Temple*, *op.cit.*, p. 73.
17. *Tantraraja Tantra* XXX, 4.f., according to Stella Kramrisch, *op.cit.*, p. 80.
18. *Samarangana Sutradhara* XIV.11, according to Stella Kramrisch, *op.cit.*, p. 79.
19. Stella Kramrisch, *op.cit.*, p. 85.
20. *Tantrasamuccaya*, *Patala* I, stanzas 4, 5, 6, according to N.V. Mallaya, *op.cit.*, p. 29.
21. The same relationship was the directive principle in Christian art up to the beginning of the Renaissance. 'His art alone belongs to the painter, its organisation and arrangement belong to clergy'. (Second Council of Nicaea, A.D. 787).
22. For an exhaustive discussion on the *Vedic* altar and its relationship to the Vimana see Stella Kramrisch, *The Hindu Temple*, *op.cit.*, p. 22 ff, p. 69 ff. A summary of this discussion is found in Titus Burckhardt, *The Genesis of the Hindu Temple*, *op.cit.*, p.

2 ff. To develop these co-respondences here would take us too far from the central theme.

23. *Shilparatna* I, 29-42, according to Stella Kramrisch, *op.cit.*, p. 10. In this connection it may be interesting to note the qualifications required from the architect according to the *Shilparatna*: 'The *Sthapati* should be fit to direct the construction and should be well-versed in all the Shastras, the traditional sciences, perfect in body, righteous, kind, free from malice and jealousy, a Tantrik, well-born; he should know mathematics and the *Puranas*, the ancient compendia of myth, etc., painting and all the countries; he should be joyous, truth speaking, with senses under control concentrated in mind, free from greed, carelessness, disease and the seven vices; famous, having firm friends and having crossed the ocean of science of *Vastu*'. One cannot but pause to wonder how the modern architect's qualifications would compare.
24. Balikarmavidhana, according to N.V. Mallaya, *op.cit.*, p. 89.
25. A.K. Coomaraswamy, *Indian Collections in the Boston Museum of Fine Arts*, Part II, p. 37.
26. *Tantrasamuccaya*, *Patala* I.21, according to N.V. Mallaya, *op.cit.*, p. 35 and commentary, p. 124.

    According to Mr. Mallaya's commentary the three points (Figs. 4- 2, 3, 4) are found by first describing a circle around the gnomon (1) with a larger radius than the gnomon's length. 'During the course of the Sun from morning till evening three points will be secured (by marking the end of the gnomon's shadow): two touching the circumference and one in the centre, the interval in the course of their marking being equal'.
27. The author of the *Tantrasamuccaya* remarks that the simpler construction described in the Manasara, relying merely upon one fish to find the north-south line, is correct only if the site lies on the Equator. This obviously special case is reproduced in Titus Burckhardt's *Principles et Méthodes de l'Art Sacré*. The construction shown here is in accordance with the text of the *Tantrasamuccaya* and in accordance with the commentary upon the text by N.V. Mallaya. The very slight asymmetry of the shadow's path about the north-south axis seems to account for the more precise method.
28. We have referred to the verticality of the Gopuram in relation to the temple wall in the first part of this study; see also Fig. 1.
29. The *fallen* shadow is analogous to the *fallen* existence (*Vastu*) from unified Being (*Sattva*). The undetermined and *asuric* nature of the 'fall' is analogous to the lack of light in the shadow.
30. It is significant to observe that the literal meaning of geometry from its Greek roots is 'measuring of the earth'.
31. *Tantrasamuccaya*, *Patala* I, stanza 22, according to N.V. Mallaya, *op.cit.*, p. 35.
32. Cf. Stella Kramrisch: *op.cit.*, p. 85 n.
33. A.K. Coomaraswamy, *Symbolism of the Dome*, *op.cit.*, p. 18 n.
34. *Ibid.*, p. 19, according to Mrs. Sinclair Stevenson, *The Rites of the Twice Born*.
35. *Shatapatha Brahmana* II.1.1.8-9, according to Coomaraswamy, *Symbolism of the Dome*, *op.cit.*, p. 21.
36. *From the Ballad of the Iron Pillar at Delhi*, according to A.K. Coomaraswamy.
37. *Jataka* V.129 f., according to A.K. Coomaraswamy, *Symbolism of the Dome*, *op.cit.*, pp. 36-37. Mr. Coomaraswamy adds: 'This is unmistakably a 'folklore' version of the

Sutraman doctrine, according to which the Sun connects these worlds and all things to himself by means of a thread of spiritual light'.

38. The considerations alluded to only briefly above are very complex and varied. For a much more exhaustive discussion on the subject see Stella Kramrisch, *op.cit.*, p. 29 ff., 40 ff., 51 ff., 85 ff. Also Titus Burckhardt, *op.cit.*, p. 7 ff. and N.V. Mallaya, pp. 127-129.
39. N.V. Mallaya, *op.cit.*, p. 130.
40. *Shilparatna* X.6-13, according to Stella Kramrisch, *op.cit.*, p. 110.
41. *Tantrasamuccaya*, Patala I, Stanza 29, according to N.V. Mallaya, *op.cit.*, p. 39.
42. Cf. Stella Kramrisch, *op.cit.*, p. 128 n.

PART IV

THE SYMBOLS OF TRANSCENDENCE

The Fourth is non-characterized: it is actionless, without any trace of the development of manifestation, abounding in Bliss and without duality: that is *Omkara*, that assuredly is *Atma*. He who knows this enters verily into his own Self by means of that same Self.

Mandukya Upanishad
Shruti 12

1. THE WOMB OF SPIRITUAL REBIRTH

Manifestation and development occurred on the measured horizontal field: immediately its limits were established and fixed, the process of gathering began. Expansion, analogous to creation, is the vehicle of multiplicity and is the result of the 'fall', but gathering, analogous to reabsorption is the way to Unity and occasions ascension; the former takes place on the horizontal plane, the latter in the vertical direction.

The extent of the raised basement (*Adhisthana*) is the limit of expansion for the Vimana. Its perimeter is a significant measure from which other important measures and proportions are derived.[1] It is the measured horizontal field from which the vertical structure grows, increasing in height but decreasing in horizontal expansion. The *Adhisthana* is the square platform on which the sacrifice of the 'Golden Purusha', the schematic man built into the temple, will take place: its pristine prototype is then no other than the Vedic altar upon which the ascending flame of the sacrificial fire 'carried' the sacrifice to the domain of the aniconic *Vedic* gods. 'The place of flame is now taken by the structure on its socle; it arises with perpendicular walls and a pointed superstructure. Neither the form of the socle with its horizontal mouldings nor that of the temple on it imply a derivation of the form of the *Agni* or its flame; but it is the knowledge of these rites which survives in architectural forms'.[2]

The visible structure of the Vimana affirms thus once again its ontological link with the *Vedic* altar, alluded to before. The expression of the form has, of course, undergone extensive change in accordance with the adverse conditions inherent in the cyclic progress, but the symbolic content remained the same. The direct sacrificial fire has been replaced by the indirect sacrificial offering (*Puja*) to the enshrined image. The once open sacrificial shed became solidly enclosed. But the basic geometrical symbols inherent in the open Vedic sacrifice, namely the horizontal plane of the altar (*Vedi*), the vertical pillar of rising flame (*Stambha*) and the dome of the sky beyond have not merely been preserved in the Vimana of Sundareswar but elaborated and emphasized to an astonishing degree; upon these basic symbolic elements rests the whole of the Vimana, as a monument, effective as a symbol in its own right if seen (*Darshana*) and understood.

Let us return to the initiatory *Vedic* sacrificial shed, the *Sadas*, 'which is covered on all sides with mats and faces the East where is its door'.[3] 'That *Sadas* they enclose on all sides with a view to that generation, thinking: Quite secretly shall be carried on that generation, for improper indeed is the generation which anyone sees. Therefore to anyone looking into the *Sadas* except through the door, let him say: 'Look not'; for it is as if he were seeing intercourse being carried on. Freely (one may look) through the door, for the door is made by the gods'.[4]

The generation refers to the spiritual rebirth of the initiator or of the sacrificer. It takes place in an enclosed space, protected from the influences of the external, profane world, since the act performed within is sacred and secret. The generation occurs within the house (*Griha*) of the germ (*Garbha*). It is the secret womb (*Garbhagriha*) in which the *new life* germinates, understood not in the physical but in the metaphysical sense. In the square, dark chamber is the germ, in the form of the *Linga*, contained; identifying himself with the germ the sacrificer is born anew and released into spiritual life, 'non-characterized' and unconditioned.

The structure erected on the *Adhisthana* consisted originally of an open space surrounded by pillars which supported the roof.

> In temples of Gods commonly (coming under the common measure type) pillars are said to be twelve in number, which should be posted above Prati (the top moulding of the basement) at the four corners and in the middle, the interstices (between pillars) being equal?[5]

The part of the temple rising above the *Adhisthana* is called *Pada* (leg) or *Stambha* (pillar), although these pillars have thickened into continuous solid walls (*Bhitti*) surrounding the *Garbhagriha* of Lord Sundareswar (Fig. 3) leaving but a single opening on the east.[6] Reference has been made before to the process of solidification and to the necessity of protecting the sanctum once open towards the, pair of horizontal axes (the north-south and east-west lines) which intersect in the point where the *Linga* is erected. In this connection one will recall that a wall is, at the same time, a protection *and* a limitation, and whilst the protective function excludes the 'infernal' influences, the same function necessarily limits the 'radiation' of the Supreme Symbol in all but one of the cardinal directions. Now, as M. Guénon remarked, the advantages of the protective function are incomparably greater than the disadvantages resulting from the necessary limitation. Nevertheless, the *Tantrasamuccaya* attempts to overcome the inherent disadvantages, at least symbolically:

> Dividing the thickness of the wall into twelve parts and giving five and seven parts outside and inside respectively mark out a line; then construct doors (*Dvaras*) on all the (four) sides above Prati, they being so situated that the middle line of their jambs (*Dvarashakhas*) coincides with the demarcating *sutra* designed, while the centre of the door is a little deviated from the centre of the *Prasada*. Excepting the front door, all will be *Ghanadvaras* which are adorned in their above with Toranas.[7]

The *Ghanadvaras* are false doors,[8] solidly built in. They form a niche on the external wall face housing the image of a deity, which is an anthropomorphic aspect of the *Linga* enshrined within. In this way the *Ghanadvaras* establish the connection between the present solidly walled-in space and the original open shrine radiating in all directions and admitting approach from east, south, west and north. The false

Pl. 14a. Tank of the Golden Lilies — the Tiruvachi Gopuram in the background

l. 14b. Tank of the Golden Lilies — the Tiruvachi and the Raya (Eastern) Gopuram in the background

Pl. 15 Colonnades around the Tank of the Golden Lilies; the South Gopura in the background

Pl. 16. Bird's eye view of the Temple looking south-east

Pl. 17a. Bird's eye view of the Temple along the main east-west axis, looking west

ll. 17b. Vishnu offering Minakshi in marriage to Sundareswar, West Gopuram, detail

Pl. 18. Bird's eye view from the top of the South Gopuram, looking north

Pl. 19. The Vimana of Sundareswar

Pl. 20. Pillars around the Tank of the Golden Lilies

doors refer and relate also to the *Gopuram*: the gate tower erected in all the cardinal directions which admit approach, at least virtually,[9] to the less sacred parts of the Shri Minakshi Sundareswar. And whilst the Supreme Symbol must not be revealed in any direction but the east, its 'radiation' is accomplished, even if on a lower level, by the anthropomorphic images housed in the *Ghanadvaras*, and ultimately by the towering Gopurams themselves.

Due to its single opening the *Garbhagriha* of Lord Sundareswar is dark, its internal walls are bare; its darkness is the primordial womb, the primordial Substance, *Prakriti*. 'In the beginning this Universe existed in the shape of darkness'.[10] 'In the beginning there was Darkness hidden in Darkness'.[11] Yet this darkness must no longer be thought of as the womb of creation, as the origin of multiplicity and manifestation. It should be transposed analogically to become the source of reintegration, 'a necessary condition for the transformation which is wrought in the devotee. In darkness his change is effected and a new life is attained'.[12] The path of re-integration reverses the process of creation. The undefined, primordial Substance has to be met with anew within the heart of the sacrificer: all his attachment to manifestation will be reabsorbed into this darkness as a precondition to spiritual rebirth. Within the bare, dark, square chamber stands the *Linga*, the supreme symbol of Shiva, the Transformer; it rests at the same time within the heart of the devotee. And whether the dark, primordial womb is thought of as within or without us, whether it is represented by the *Garbhagriha*, or spoken of as the city of Brahma, or again as a small cavity in the heart, its meaning is always the source of spiritual reintegration. 'In this city of Brahma is a small lotus, a dwelling in which is a small cavity occupied by ether (*Akasha*). That which lies in this place should be though after and one will know it'.[13]

The vertical element rising from the *Adhisthana* is named *Pada* (leg) or *Sthamba* (pillar). These pillars have given up their independent existence and have now become continuous walls surrounding the *Garbhagriha*; they are found, however, in superabundance around the Vimana, forming the several surrounding Mandapams of the temple. Their significance, related to the central theme of the Vimana, is contingent; however, on account of their ontological link with the *Garbhagriha* and also on account of their overwhelming architectural effect in the surrounding Mandapams (Pl. 20), a brief examination of their meaning will not be out of place here.

As a vertical element extending between the two horizontal limits of an enclosed space, the prototype of the pillar is the *Vedic* 'pillar of fire' rising from the earthly plane of the altar towards the dome of the sky. In one sense the earth (*Bhu*) and the sky (*Swar*) correspond to the lower and the higher domains of manifestation, namely to the sensible and to the causal world respectively, but in another sense Heaven and Earth correspond to the two principles of manifestation, Essence and Substance. In this latter sense the totality of manifestation develops between its two indefinitely removed limits and comprises all the three worlds (*Triloka*), the causal, the ideal, and the sensible. The pillar thus becomes the vertical axis which establishes the connection between the several orders of existence and also between the several states of the being, and it is in this sense that *Agni* is 'a pillar supporting the kindreds'[14] and that 'He is a pillar of life at the parting of the ways'[15] and 'Heaven and Earth the pillars apart'.[16] Further, it should not be overlooked that the Buddha is represented in numerous cases as a fiery pillar,[17] and relates in more than one aspect to the Tree of Life and the Axis of the Universe. 'The wood was Brahma, Brahma the tree of which they fashioned Heaven and Earth; it is my deliberate word, ye knowledgeable men, that there stands Brahma world supporting'.[18]

The pillar, regarded in itself, coincides then with the Axis of the Universe no matter where it stands.[19] It is planted on the earth, generally symbolized by the lotus (*Padma*), hence its base (*Oma*) retains lotus-petal mouldings (Fig. 3 and Pl. 20). According to the *Tantrasamuccaya* it may be four, eight or sixteen sided, or a combination of all these, related to the directions of space, and rises through three parts (*Ghata*, *Mandi*, *Virakanda*) to end in the capital (*Potika*). It has then altogether five parts or nodes which correspond to the five nodes (*Chakras*) of the human body and to the three worlds plus two poles of universal manifestation. Its lotus-bud-capital and lotus-petal-base represent the powers derived from the Celestial or Upper Waters and from the Terrestrial or Nether Waters, to which *Vastu-Shastras* possibilities' we have alluded before. 'As the Nether Lotus is the Earth, the substance of things, so the Conch or Upper Lotus is their form; in other words, while the lower symbols stand for means or ground of utterance, the upper symbols stand for the power of utterance, all that is uttered coming into existence between them'.[20]

One could extend almost indefinitely, by citing texts from the *Shruti* and *Smriti*, the connections that exist between the pillar, the Tree of Life, the *Vedic* sacrificial post, the axle-tree of the chariot-wheels, the Axis of the Universe, and the vertical arm of the three-dimensional cross. Considering that the Shri Minakshi Sundareswar has several thousand pillars, nearly all different in their iconography, and that they have all been built according to strictly described proportions given in the *Vastu-Shastras*, it is easy to see that the foregoing discussion aimed merely to relate the pillar to the central theme of the Vimana rather than to *devel*op its significance, as an independent symbol, fully. The pillars, regarded in themselves, are merely contingent applications of the symbolism which finds its position *par excellence* attached to the central shaft (*Venu*) of the Vimana, around which axis the entire temple 'revolves'. It will then be appropriate to return to Lord Sundareswar's shrine and examine in ascending order the parts of its superstructure.

The entablature (*Prastara*) covering the *Garbhagriha* is made up of heavy stone beams and thick, flat stone slabs. Over this is the pyramidal superstructure erected in two storeys (*Bhumi*). They consist of an externally invisible solid core surrounded by richly sculptured miniature temples, each a replica of the early open shrine, each housing an image and covered with a dome. Occurring as they do over the level of the earth, the two *Bhumis* can be looked upon as representing the levels or degrees of the ideal states of manifestation. The twelve miniature temples are the higher reflections of the twelve columns encountered before, supposedly surrounding the *Garbhagriha*, but existing only virtually within its solid wall. Quite apart from the possible astrological considerations resting on the signs of the Zodiac, one is faced here again with a protective tendency afforded by the twelve shrines to the central shaft.[21]

The architectural arrangement and the symbolism of the *Bhumis* is very similar to that of the Gopuram, which structure is, as it were, an externalized replica of the Vimana itself. There are, however, divergencies between these two monuments; the discrepancies all seem to show that the perfect shape of the central shrine is the sacred prototype of the imperfect and externalized shape of the gate. The most significant differences arise from the rectangular base of the Gopuram as compared to the square base of the Vimana. The square, as the most determined and arrested shape of all planar shapes, reflecting the immutability of the Principle, is perfect in its symmetry compared to the imperfect and undetermined relationship of the unequal sides of the rectangle. Based on the square, the superstructure of the Vimana emphasizes no direction to the detriment of another; it is the centre of all directions. Based on the rectangle, the Gopuram differentiates between the longer and shorter sides; it is therefore directional. The directions of the surrounding walls find their accentuation on the longer side of the rectangular base, thus depriving the Gopuram from independence of its surroundings which a perfectly symmetrical shape alone enjoys.

The central, projecting buttresses found only on the two opposite sides of the Gopuram appear on all the four faces of the superstructure of the Vimana. Nor do these buttresses repeat openings on each floor, since the basic symbolism of the gate is no longer appropriate here, neither in any case, in the horizontal sense: the Vimana *is* the centre to which all horizontal directions lead. The buttresses, whose projecting part appears on the ground plan, relate not so much to the centre line of the triangle seen in elevation as to the two main orthogonals of the square plan, trancing the horizontal cross. The directionless centre is affirmed once again: the Gopurams are the gate through which the directional way leads, the Vimana is the core to which all movement arrives.

Over the shoulder course (*Skandha*) of the ever-receding pyramidal levels, where the continuous recession is stopped and the pyramid is truncated, emerges visibly for the first time the central shaft (*Venu*) of the Vimana; it forms the neck (*Griva*) of the total superstructure and, at the same time, the walls of the High Temple (*Harmya Prasada*) erected over the shoulder course. The High Temple is the structure in which the pyramidal recession of the *Bhumis* terminates; it appears only over the Vimana and does not form part of Gopurams. It rejoins, symbolically, the High Altar (*Uttara Vedi*) of the *Vedic* sacrificial ground to which the sacrificial fire was carried over from the lower altars for the purpose of the highest sacrifice.[22] Its shape is again reminiscent of the early, open shrines; its meaning stands for the highest orders of manifestation, the formless or causal world. These orders of existence – proceeding from the gross level of the earth through the subtle levels of the *Bhumis* to the formless order of the High Temple – must no longer be considered purely in the outward, the macrocosmic sense: they are the states of the Golden Person who is built into the temple, or rather, whose form the temple imitates. His germ, placed into the ground has come to life in the darkness of the womb. He is built into the structure as a holocaust, facing the sky, and with him the spiritual seeker identifies himself treading the path of re-integration. Rising, the extension and expansion inherent in existence are gradually left behind, and the process, analogous to contraction or concentration, leads to the attainment of the extra-corporeal modalities of the subtle state and to the supra-individual, that is, the supra-formal states, represented by the *Bhumis* and the High Temple respectively. Whether viewed from .the macrocosmic point as the several states of the Being, the receding levels of the Vimana gather from all the directions the multiplicity of manifestation towards the principal Unity which is its source.

2. THE AXIS OF THE UNIVERSE

The High Temple of Lord Sundareswar's shrine is covered by a golden entablature and a golden four-faced dome. This is the *Shikara* (head) of the Vimana, the form which finally gathers up the fourfold extension of existence (*Vastu*) represented in the *Vastupurusha-Mandala.* The independent existence of and all opposition between the four faces ceases in the crown of the dome; it is pierced, in turn, by the *Stupika.*

The sacrifice *in divinis* represented by the fundamental procedure from Unity to quadrature – which sacred act 'was' performed for the 'sake' of contingent beings – is now reversed by the human sacrifice, by returning from quadrature to Unity. And as the separation of principal Unity implied a 'break' much the same way the process of unification cannot be achieved by continuous, gradual concentration: the pyramidal form is truncated and the final unification is achieved by the dome rising above the levels of formal and formless manifestation. By the four-faced dome the square of Lord Sundareswar's Vimana is brought back to the dimensionless point from which it arose; the multiplicity of all degrees of existence merge once more into the unity of Principal Being (*Ishwara*).

By envisaging this unification of the contingent being with principal Being, the metaphysic of the Hindu doctrine is far from being complete. In fact, its most important considerations transcend Being, since this Principle, immensely exalted as it may be from the ordinary human point of view, is nevertheless qualified (*Saguna*) and limited compared to the truly unqualified (*Nirguna*) and absolutely unlimited Infinity of Brahma. Therefore it is not surprising to see that the Vimana is not completed by the curve of the dome since this shape implies a limit, an enclosure or a shell preventing any communication with domains situated beyond it. Only by opening up the possibility of reaching beyond Being can the symbolism of the dome become profound.[23]

One will recall at this juncture that the barrel vaulted roof of the Gopuram was pierced by 'arrows', 'shafts', or 'axes', and one may add that their multiplicity fore-shadowed in an inferior way the single shaft *par excellence* (*Venu*), much the same way as many other aspects of the Gopuram externalized in an imperfect mode the perfection of the Vimana. It is important to understand that the *Venu*, to which several references were made before, is not built actually and continuously throughout the Vimana, but exists, nevertheless, virtually; it rises directly above the gnomon which was its pristine prototype, regulates the symmetry of the structure of which it is the axis, is encased into the rising pyramidal superstructure, becomes visible in the neck (*Griva*) and finally, pierces the dome (*Stupika*). The elements of the *Stupika*, namely the full-blown lotus (*Padma*), pot (*Kumbha*), stalk (*Nala*), and top in the form of a fresh lotus bud (*Kudmala*) (Fig. 3) have all definite meanings to be discerned before the symbolism of the dome could be fully developed.

The lotus (*Padma*) is explicitly 'full-blown' and eight-petalled, corresponding to the 'upper lotus', 'The one lotus on the zenith'[24] having solar characteristics: it could even be assimilated to the Sun itself. Recalling the symbolism of the pillar, where the same 'upper lotus' formed a correlation with the 'lotus of the earth', and also the rituals preceding the construction of the temple, when the 'lower lotus' was deposited, it becomes clear that this 'Celestial Lotus' with its petals turned downwards forms the complementary principle of the 'Earthly Lotus' upon which the temple rests. It represents 'the celestial region where the rays of the sun spread like the filaments of the lotus of the zenith'[25] and showers its beneficial effect upon the earth.

Over the lotus is the pot (*Kumbha* or *Kalasha*) mostly considered or actually built in an inverted position. This High Vase is again the counterpart of the Low Vase which was installed under the structure containing the treasures of the Earth or the germs of the Golden *Purusha*, which the total temple as a symbol represents. '*Vishvakarma* made the *Kalasha* (High Vase) from the different parts of each of the gods'.[26] 'So the substance of the *Kalasha*, which is gold, as a rule, contains the properties of each of the gods up in the deathless region, straight above the *Nidhi-Kalasha* (Low Vase) in the foundation of the temple, in which were placed the treasures of the earth. The treasures would be transmuted into Deathlessness in the High Vase, in which their several colours, scents and shapes would have entered through their presiding divinities. As above the temple so also is a vase below the temple'.[27] At the consecration ceremony into this vase the Golden *Purusha* is installed.

Beyond the symbolism implied by the complementary aspects of the High Vase and the Low Vase, the golden *Kalasha* is also directly connected to the sun: 'The golden *Kalasha*, a high seat on the summit of the gods' dwelling, looks as if it were the sun's orb that had arisen on the lordly mountain of sunrise'.[28] In this connection one will have to consider the question 'Who is qualified to pass through the midst of the Sun?'[29] Because 'through the hub of the wheel, the midst of the Sun, the cleft in heaven, that is all covered over by rays, that one is altogether liberated',[30] and also through the rays of the Sun 'Of which, *one* standeth upward, breaking through the solar orb and overpassing into the Brahma-world, thereby men attain their final goal'.[31]

The foregoing considerations and quotations helped to shed light upon the meaning of the central shaft (*Venu*) of the Vimana from two different aspects. Firstly, the symbolism of the High and Low Lotus and the High and Low Vase – the ones situated below turning upwards and the ones situated above turning downwards – establishes the two poles of the connecting axis; both these poles are outside the Vimana proper, that is outside manifestation, and it is *between* them that all degrees of existence come into being. These poles are assimilated then to *Purusha* and *Prakriti*, or to Heaven and Earth, and the axis, which 'pillars Heaven and Earth apart' is none other than the Axis of the Universe, which axis connects, but at the same time separates, the two complementary principles of manifestation; along this axis the horizontal planes of the several degrees of existence become conditioned, determined and 'measured'. From this point of view the central shaft is also the vertical arm of the three-dimensional cross, to which we shall presently return.

From another point of view the *Venu* is the ray of the Sun, the *one* which 'standeth upward', and it is precisely this ray which breaks through the solar disc, now identified with the *Kalasha*, or even with the apex of the dome. The solar disc – just as Tvastri's unquartered cup and the dome – is eminently symbolic of principal Unity, or Being, and only by breaking through this seemingly complete barrier that 'men attain their final goal'. The dome of the Vimana is not enclosed as no dome built on traditional principles can ever be:[32] it is pierced through by the shaft (*Venu*), the one Heavenly Ray, rising directly from the *Linga*, from the darkness of the *Garbhagriha*. Into this darkness the 'ingress is horizontal, the egress vertical'[33] and the 'generation of the new life' – which results from the extinction of the old life – follows the Heavenly Ray directly through the several states of the being. However, 'the stations on the way to Brahma are conductors of the soul, not marks of the road nor places of enjoyment'[34] – the Ray must be followed through, past the unity of the dome past the disc of the sun 'where no sun shines', that is, beyond manifestation, beyond even Being into the absolutely unconditioned state of Brahma.

The shaft of Lord Sundareswar's Vimana ends in a lotus bud (*Kudmala*, *Bindu*), the point limit between manifestation and the Unmanifest, since nothing ever can directly symbolize That. Yet this physical ending affects neither the symbol as it is *seen* (*Darshana*) nor its meaning. The tremendous rising verticality built up by the richly carved pyramidal layers and the dome, running right through the internal shaft will inevitably escape through its 'limit', just as the bud, rising from the full-blown lotus is indicative of another, of an incomprehensible flowering beyond, just as the indefinite prolongation of the sacred monosyllable *OM* refers to the 'non-characterized' state of *ATMA*, one's 'own Self' entered 'by means of that same Self'.

3. THE THREE-DIMENSIONAL CROSS

The *Venu* of the Vimana regarded as the Axis of the Universe – a meaning which was temporarily left behind – establishes a symbolism of another kind, leading to the self-same end through somewhat different considerations. This is what may be called the symbolism of the cross, but its complex metaphysical applications arising from purely geometrical considerations must remain outside the central theme of this study.[35] However, the symbol of the three-dimensional cross will give rise to a synthesis, not merely of all the aspects connected to the Vimana, but also of those which determine the entire layout of the Shri Minakshi Sundareswar.

The three-dimensional cross made its appearance during the very first operation of the Stapathi when he fixed the *Vastupurusha-Mandala* of the temple: there the vertical gnomon erected at the origo was the 'efficient cause' of the subsequently determined east-west and north-south axes lying on the horizontal plane. These three axes intersecting at the origo form a trihedral right angle and their indefinite extension in the three dimensions – or the six directions – of space form the three-dimensional cross. The symbolism of this basic figure[36] can be considered from a multitude of points of view[37] each of which can lead to complex applications. However, first it will be necessary to consider the relationship of the elements of the basic figure in the general sense, leaving the possibility open for particular symbolic applications.

The two horizontal axes of the cross define a horizontal plane at right angles to the vertical axis. In the case of the Vimana this plane coincides with the surface of the ground upon which the whole expansion took place; it serves as the support to the vertical superstructure of the temple. Any horizontal plane, necessarily defined by two axes, can then be regarded as a 'ground' upon which development of a kind will take place.

This last loose terminology is adopted here intentionally so that the idea of 'development' should no longer remain attached to the example of the temple we used, nor even to the limitations of the corporeal order. Nevertheless, any development which takes place on any horizontal plane will be limited by certain conditions. A horizontal plane is regarded then in a general sense as–a 'field' upon which development is limited by certain conditions. Within the limiting conditions, however, the possibilities are indefinite, hence the plane must be thought of as extending indefinitely in both directions of its two axes. It represents then a double indefinitude – or the indefinite to the power of two – whilst any *one* of the axes represents a simple indefinitude – or the indefinite to the power of one.

Another set of conditions determining another kind of development must be represented by another horizontal plane which will be situated higher or lower relative to the first one, that is, its position will be moved along the vertical axis. Once an indefinite number of sets of conditions is conceived an indefinite number of horizontal planes will follow. Each of these planes is intersected by the connecting vertical axis, and this point of intersection is the centre of the plane and the origin of the two axes defining the plane.[38] The three-dimensional cross is then capable of representing triple indefinitude – or the indefinite to the power of three – which, in turn, is contained in the volume of an indefinitely extended sphere of which the polar and the two equatorial axes coincide with the vertical and the two horizontal axes of the cross.

The three-dimensional cross, of course, will be very often represented on a plane surface as a projection (Fig. 6). It can be viewed along its vertical axis, in which case the vertical axis will become a point at the rectangular intersection of two lines of equal length (a); it can be viewed along a given horizontal plane, in which case the two axes originally contained in the plane will coincide into a single horizontal line curtailed relative to the vertical (b); again, it can be viewed from a non-specific position, in which case all the three axes will appear in the projection (c), and the figure will be the prototype of the six-pointed star (d).

The equal length of the two arms of the first case indicates that both axes were situated in the horizontal plane, that is, in the same relative position to the vertical axis; however, one arm will inevitably assume a verticality relative to the other. The unequal length of the second case indicates that the vertical arm represents the original vertical axis in its projection. In the third case the verticality of the original vertical axis is naturally retained.

The foregoing description attempted to present the symbol in a general sense which does not exclude any of its possible applications either in the physical or in the metaphysical domains. Our aim is not to consider each or some of these possible applications, but to develop the one which is related to the central theme of this study. The relation is the vertical axis of the Vimana as the Axis of the Universe, which arose from the symbolism of the Lower and Higher Lotus and the Lower and Higher Vase; they were assimilated before to the poles of manifestation, to universal Substance and Essence respectively.

Between the two indefinitely removed poles of the vertical axis will the whole of the manifestation enfold; each horizontal plane will represent then *one degree of existence* participating in universal Essence and Substance in proportions appropriate to its situation. The sum of all such horizontal planes comprises all degrees of existence, that is, universal manifestation. One of the indefinite number of horizontal planes will represent the degree of human existence upon which we, as human beings, are situated and governed by the conditions defining the position of this one plane relative to the others. This position is special only from the human point of view – a point of view one will necessarily adopt as long as one is situated within the plane – but it is obvious that from a purely metaphysical point of view such distinction cannot be made. However, to enable our defining the three-dimensional cross, a particular horizontal plane must be regarded as *given* and from the human point of view it will be inevitable to relate all other horizontal planes – that is all other degrees of existence – to our own, situated either above or below the position we occupy.

Now, any horizontal plane, but in particular the one corresponding to human existence, is defined by two axes, forming the two-dimensional cross. Each of these axes represents a single indefinitude: one corresponds to the indefinitude of the individuals, the other to that of the different modalities which the individuals are capable of developing in the one degree of human existence. Similarly, all other horizontal planes are defined by two axes corresponding analogically to the

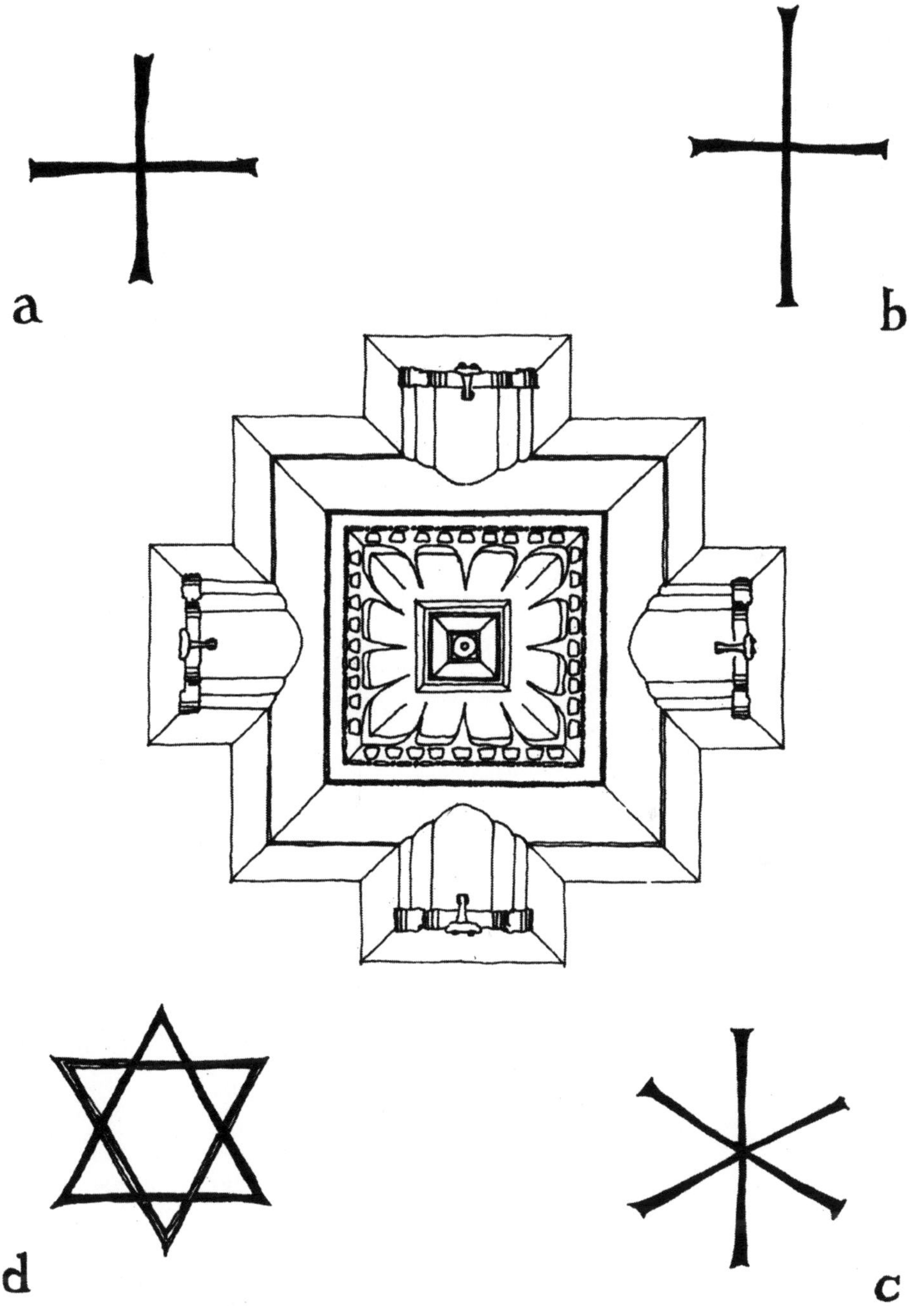

Fig. 6. Vimana of Sundareswar, top view (in centre), and symbols of the cross

indefinitudes just mentioned, but appropriate to any other particular degree of existence.

All the degrees of existence are linked together by the Axis of the Universe, which can be spoken of also as the 'Will of Heaven'[39] or the 'Celestial Ray'.[40] Its intersection with each horizontal plane determines the 'centre' of the 'field', since this point is the reflection of the axis as a whole upon the plane; it is the origo, the efficient as well as the material cause of all development peculiar to the particular horizontal plane.

The Vimana, as the whole structure, will then acquire a meaning somewhat different to the one we have attributed to its superstructure when developing the symbolism of the dome. From the present point of view the Vimana represents manifestation as a whole; the ground level corresponds to the one degree of human existence (which includes some possibilities of the corporeal as well as of the subtle order, both limited by form), the levels of the superstructure to the degrees of existence situated above the human one, and the levels of the substructure to the degrees of existence situated below. The central shaft of the Vimana, the Axis of the Universe, must be thought of as penetrating into the ground below earth level, as indeed it does by piercing the Serpent's head; it goes through the foundation pit, through all the symbols built into the ground, and links all the rituals attached to them. The substructure of the Vimana is then just as important as its visible superstructure; it represents degrees of existence that are situated below and 'support' the human level, much the same way as human existence is the 'support' of all the levels situated above it. We have now adopted a point of view in which the degree of human existence tends to lose its special significance, occupying just one level in the whole of manifestation represented by the total volume of the Vimana.

The centre of the whole of manifestation, which coincides with the origo of the three-dimensional cross, is universal Being (*Ishwara*); He must no longer be sought after as situated 'somewhere above' but, indeed in the centre, in the origo of the three-dimensional cross. From the absolute point of view this centre is potentially everywhere (since any vertical axis can be regarded as *the* axis and any horizontal plane contains the other two axes), but from a human point of view the centre *is* where the three axes of the *Vastupurusha-Mandala* meet. And it is precisely at this point that the *Linga*, the supreme symbol of Shiva, is installed, approached and worshipped. Its round shaft coincides – in position and in meaning – with the Axis of the Universe.

If one would project this entire three-dimensional complex upon a horizontal surface – that is, represent the three-dimensional cross as a two-dimensional cross (Fig. 6, a) – then the horizontal plane would no longer represent a single degree of existence but the totality of all degrees of existence. This case is identical with the symbolism of the unique Wheel (*Chakra*), which is fundamental to all eastern traditions. Here the manifested worlds are represented by the felly which is peripheral in relation to the motionless central point around which it revolves.

Without going into the further details of this symbol, equally capable of manifold extension, we will be concerned solely with its application to our case.

The view in question corresponds to the top view of the Vimana (Fig. 6, centre), but in addition to this to the top view of the entire temple, which coincides with its plan (Fig. 2). The circumference, made up of a succession of concentric circles in the case of the wheel, appears in the case of the temple in the form of successively diminishing concentric squares. Each of these represents a single degree of *existence* in indefinite continuity. The centre is once more the totality of Being and the radii, which connect the centre to any point on the periphery, correspond to the 'Celestial Ray' of the Sun spoken of to 'string these worlds to Him by the thread of the Gale of Spirit'.[41] The devotee, who circumambulates the temple, moves on the ground of the entire manifestation[42] where each and every point is connected to the Supernal Sun as 'rows of gems on a string'. During his progress the sacrificer will seek to identify himself with the 'thread' (which, in a microcosmic sense, corresponds to the 'higher intellect', *Buddhi*), whence his progress to Unity becomes radial, 'direct', instead of remaining peripheral, 'indirect'.[43]

In the foregoing description the two arms of the horizontal cross were assimilated into the indefinite number of rays radiating from the centre. However, it is inevitable that one of the arms of the horizontal cross will assume a verticality relative to the other, and will represent, in a certain sense, the symbolism attached to the vertical axis of the three-dimensional cross. The layout of the Shri Minakshi Sundareswar (Fig. 2) shows clearly the two-dimensional cross connecting the four outermost Gopurams, and emphasizes unmistakably the east-west axis in relation to the north-south; the former assumes an 'essentiality' in relation to the latter's 'substantiality'. From this last aspect, the east-west axis is the Axis of the Universe, which 'pillars Heaven and Earth apart' and the five Gopurams situated on this axis are analogous in a sense to the five parts of the column, to the five nodes, or Chakras, of the human body, to the three worlds (*Triloka*) plus two poles of manifestation, to all of which we have alluded earlier. In relation to this axis the north-south line will be regarded as a projection of a plane of existence; their intersection corresponding, of course, to principal Being, is marked by the Vimana of Lord Sundareswar.

One could object that the north-south-axis of the Vimana does not coincide exactly with the centre just referred to, but is situated further to the west. Instead of attempting to consider further complexities of the two superimposed crosses, of two Vimanas fused into Unity, one will recall that, no matter where or when a temple is built on traditional principles, it must never exhibit the ideal geometrical state.[44] The Vimana of Lord Sundareswar coincides *virtually* with the centre of the temple and the *Linga* is not merely the vertical axis of the Vimana but also of the whole of the Shri Minakshi Sundareswar.

This supreme symbol of Shiva synthesizes in its laconic form all that has been said before. It emerges from – but penetrates at the same time the *Yoni*, its complementary principle, the 'substantial' pedestal whose horizontal surface is square. Oriented towards the cardinal directions the *Yoni* is the *measured* ground of existence, the *Vastupurusha-Mandala*. It receives its measure from the heavenly circle, which circle is the cross-section of the *Linga* it holds. The two horizontal axes of the *Yoni* intersect in the vertical axis, the Axis of the Universe, the Celestial Ray: the *Linga* itself. Their common point is the efficient as well as material cause of the universe, the dimensionless unity of principal Being. In this point all separateness ceases: the *divine sacrifice* is here reiterated by the sacrifice of man.

Principal Being contains all manifestation; the three-dimensional cross of the *Linga* and the *Yoni* traces the whole of the manifested worlds. However, the passing beyond manifestation – which is the highest aim of Hindu metaphysic (deliverance, *Moksha*) – is not contained in the symbolism of the cross. The six-pointed star of the Sun (Fig. 6, c) needs a 'seventh ray which alone passes through the Sun to the supra-solar Brahma worlds 'where no sun shines' '.[45] This 'best ray'[46] which can only be spoken of as the 'solar orb itself'[47] is the symbolic Shiva in his highest aspect, bursting forth from the point of intersection of the *Linga* and the *Yoni*, as related in the Puranas.

One should refrain from an attempt to interpret this highest, this evidently supra-rational aspect of Shiva calling for insights and understandings one may not possess. The occasion calls, rather, for rejoining the traditional texts which were the basis of this study at its start. The story is related now by Brahma himself[48] in answer to an inquiry of the gods and Rishis:

In the night of Brahma when all beings and all worlds are resolved together in one equal and inseparable stillness, I beheld the great Narayana, soul of the universe, thousand eyed, omniscient, Being and non-Being alike, reclining on the formless waters, supported by the thousand headed serpent *Ananta* (Infinite); and I, deluded by his glamour, touched the eternal being with my hand and asked: 'Who art thou? Speak'. Then he of the lotus-eyes looked upon me with drowsy glance, then rose and smiled, and said: 'Welcome, my child, though shining grandsire'. But I took offence thereat and said: 'Dost thou, O sinless god, like a teacher to a pupil, call me child, who am the cause of creation and destruction, former of the myriad worlds, the source and soul of all? Tell me why dost thou thus speak foolish words to me?' Then Vishnu answered: 'Knowest thou not that I am Narayana creator, preserver and destroyer of the worlds, the eternal male, the undying source and centre of the universe? For thou wert born from my own imperishable body.

Now ensued an angry argument between us twain upon that formless sea. Then for the ending of our contention there appeared before us a glorious shining *Lingam*, a fiery pillar, like a hundred universe-consuming fires, without beginning, middle or end, incomparable, indescribable. The divine Vishnu, bewildered by its thousand flames, said unto me, who was as much astonished as himself: 'Let us forthwith seek to know this fire's source. I will descend; do thou ascend with all thy power'. Then he became a boar, like a mountain of blue collyrium, a thousand leagues in width, with white sharp pointed tusks, long-snouted, loud-grunting, short of foot, victorious, strong, incomparable – and plunged below. For a thousand years he sped thus downward, but found no base at all of the *Lingam*. Meanwhile I became a swan, white and fiery eyed, with wings on every side, swift as thought and as the wind; and I went upward for a thousand years seeking to find the pillar's end, but found it not. Then I returned and met the great Vishnu, weary and astonished, on his upward way.

Then Shiva stood before us, and we whom his magic had guiled bowed unto him, while there arose about on every hand the articulate sound of *OM*, clear and lasting. To him Narayana said: 'Happy has been our strife, thou God of gods, forasmuch as thou has appeared to end it'. Then Shiva answered to Vishnu: 'Thou art indeed the creator, preserver and destroyer of the worlds; do thou my child, maintain this world both moving and inert. For I, the undivided Overlord, am three, am Brahma, Vishnu, and Rudra, who create, maintain and destroy. Cherish this Brahma, for he shall be born of thee in an ensuing age. Then shall ye twain behold myself again'. Therewith the Great God vanished. Thereafter has the worship of the *Lingam* been established in the three worlds.

NOTES AND REFERENCES

1. Cf. *Tantrasamuccaya*, *Patala* II, stanza 3, according to N.V. Mallaya, *op.cit.*, p. 41: '*Yoni* is the remainder that results when the perimeter is multiplied by three and this product divided by eight'. According to this treatise the *Yoni* is a qualitative indicator of the Vimana according to which the orientation is decided. There can be eight *Yonis*, since the remainder can be 1, 2, 3, 4, 5, 6, 7 or 0. 'Of these, the odd *yonis* are beneficent, the even ones adverse' (*ibid.*).
2. Stella Kramrisch, *op.cit.*, p. 146.
3. Stella Kramrisch, *op.cit.*, p. 157.
4. *Shatapatha Brahmana* IV, 6, 7, 9, according to Stella Kramrisch, *op.cit.*, p. 157.
5. *Tantrasamuccaya*, *Patala* II, stanza 23, N.V. Mallaya, *op.cit.*, p. 49.
6. Nor is this an exceptional case: 'In all examples of existing sanctums regular pillars are conspicuous by their absence and their structural function of bearing the beams and the load above is carried out by the element of walls that enter into the composition of the main shrine'. (N.V. Mallaya, *op.cit.*, p. 210.)
7. *Tantrasamuccaya*, *Patala* II, stanza 26, N.V. Mallaya *op.cit.*, p. 51.
8. The centre lines of the real door as well as of the false doors must not coincide with the centre line of the Vimana. They are shifted slightly from the centre to avoid what is known as *Marmavedha.* Nor does this shift apply solely to the Vimana proper: the entire ground plan of the Shri Minakshi Sundareswar shows clearly that no axis or centre line coincides exactly with another. The avoidance of mechanical rigidity is a common characteristic of most traditional buildings, but the reasons behind it are less easily discernible. The word *Marma* means 'vulnerable spots' and *Vedha* means 'piercing'. The *Vastu-Shastras* refer to *Marma* in connection with the *Vastupurusha-Mandala* where the intersection of the diagonals with the orthogonals of the 8 x 8 or 9 x 9 divisions of the basic square are the vulnerable spots of the body of *Vastupurusha* supporting the temple. These intersections are to be avoided; doors, walls or pillars should not be built upon them. This is achieved by shifting the position of the respective parts of the building 'to the right of the vulnerable points'. (*Vastuvidya*, VI.3-7). The *Linga* should not be placed exactly in the centre of the *Garbhagriha* but slightly north-east of it, 'at the distance of half a barley corn or a barley corn in order to avoid the piercing of the centre'. (*Agnipurana*, XCVII.4.5.) Stella Kramrisch adds: 'By this slight deviation the rules of the *Vastupurusha-Mandala* are obeyed and mechanical symmetry is being avoided'. We would extend these

remarks by saying that the ideal geometry which rules the sensible form of the temple must never *appear* to coincide with it, since the sensible order is necessarily lower than the ideal from which it derives. Moreover, the appearance of coincidence, as it is the building practice of the modern West, will always be false no matter to what *degree* of refinement are the necessary *tolerances* worked to. Similarly, natural forms never coincide with the ideal mathematical formulae which they approximate. (Cf. D'Arcy Wentworth Thompson, *On Growth and Form*, 1919). Discrepancy, remainder or residue seems to underlie all existence; 'Name and Form are in the Residue. The world is in the Residue. Indra and *Agni* are in the Residue. The Universe is in the Residue'. (*Atharva Veda*, XI.9.1.)

9. At the time of the author's visit only two of the outermost Gopurams stood open, the northern and western ones excluding approach from what appears the two less favourable directions.
10. *Manu Smriti*, I.5, according to Stella Kramrisch, *op.cit.*, p. 164.
11. *Rig-Veda*, X.129.3.
12. Stella Kramrisch, *op.cit.*, p. 164.
13. *Chandogya Upanishad*, VIII.1.1., according to Stella Kramrisch, *op.cit.*, p. 164.
14. *Rig-Veda*, I.59.1, according to A.K. Coomaraswamy, *Elements of Buddhist Iconography*, Harvard University Press, Cambridge, Mass., 1935, p. 65n.
15. *Rig-Veda*, X.5.6., *ibid.*
16. *Rig-Veda*, V.29.4, *ibid.*
17. Cf. A.K. Coomaraswamy, *ibid.*, p. 10 and Fig. 1, 4-10.
18. *Taitt. Br.*II.8.9, 6, according to Bosch, *op.cit.*, pp. 65-93.
19. It seems needless to point out that the Axis of the Universe – much the same way as the Navel of the Earth or the Head of the Serpent – must not be thought of as fixed in space; all these terms denote Principles unaffected not only by spatial conditions which govern merely the sensible order, but by all the conditions governing manifestation in its totality.
20. A.K. Coomaraswamy, *Elements of Buddhist Iconography*, *op.cit.*, p. 77 n.
21. Stella Kramrisch sees the prototype of the miniature chapels in the early hypaethral temples having a central court surrounded by a row of single cells, each housing an image of one of the 64 Yoginis. Fah Hian and Hiuen Tsiang described very early Buddhist monasteries conforming to this arrangement. Vestiges of the same tendency are visible around the external wall of the Shri Minakshi Sundareswar.
22. A prolonged discussion of the *Vedic* sacrificial ritual would take us too far from our theme. For a fuller exposition see Titus Burckhardt, *op.cit.*, pp. 3-5, and Stella Kramrisch, *op.cit.*, pp. 22-29; 'The *Vedi* is the earth, the *Uttara-Vedi* the heaven world'. (*Shatapatha Brahmana*, VII.3.1.27.)
23. For an extensive treatment of this subject, embracing several traditions see the magnificent monograph of A.K. Coomaraswamy, Symbolism of the Dome, *The Indian Historical Quarterly*, March 1938.
24. *Brihadaranyaka Upanishad*, VI.3.6, according to A.K. Coomaraswamy, Symbolism of the Dome, *op.cit.*, p. 33.
25. Stella Kramrisch, *op.cit.*, p. 351.
26. *Mahanirvana Tantra*, V. 181, according to Stella Kramrisch, *op.cit.*, p. 349.
27. Stella Kramrisch, *op.cit.*, p. 350.
28. Kanarese inscription narrating the building of the Mahadeva Temple at Ittagi, A.D. 1112, according to Stella Kramrisch, *op.cit.*, p. 355.

29. *Jaiminiya Upanishad Brahmana* I.6.1, according to A.K. Coomaraswamy, Symbolism of the Dome, *op.cit.*, p. 44.
30. *Ibid.*, I. 3.5-6.
31. *Maitri Upanishad*, VI.30, *ibid.*, p. 47.
32. One will recall the innumerable examples, eastern or western, built always with an 'eye', shaft, or even completely open, before the modern era.
33. A.K. Coomaraswamy, Symbolism of the Dome, *op.cit.*, p. 14.
34. *Vedanta Sutra*, Comm.IV.III.2-7, according to Stella Kramrisch, *op.cit.*, p. 349.
35. For a comprehensive exposition see René Guénon, *The Symbolism of the Cross*, Luzac & Co., 1958. This important general work is to a great extent the source of the following particular applications.
36. The word 'figure' is used with hesitation here, since there is nothing corporeal about the three-dimensional cross. Its three axes have only one dimension and thus lie outside corporeal manifestation; it is situated, properly speaking, in the ideal state.
37. The simplest and most direct application of this ideal figure is found in solid geometry determining the directions of height, width and breadth. Further, it is the idea behind the Cartesian co-ordinates in analytical geometry and also in determining the relative positions of bodies in space. Its many applications in mathematics, physics and chemistry are well known. It is fundamental in the fields of architecture, even in certain theories of colour. We have taken the opportunity to enumerate a few *symbolic* applications of the three-dimensional cross to show that a fundamental symbol is adaptable to an indefinite number of aspects. And *symbolic* we say assuredly since there is nothing *real* connecting its ideal state to any of its applications. In this light the metaphysical point of view will seem less far-fetched for those who became used to this symbol in one or other of its contingent applications.
38. In this description we have assumed the vertical axis as *given* to avoid very far-reaching metaphysical complications. Unless this axis is given the centre of the horizontal plane cannot be determined. Inversely, without a *given* horizontal plane the centre of the vertical axis, which at the same time is the centre of the whole system, remains undefined. The centre thus is everywhere from the intrinsic point of view and nowhere from the extrinsic point of view. This is another example which shows that without assuming a given relative position no symbol has any meaning.
39. 'The vertical axis thus represents the metaphysical locus of the manifestation of the 'Will of Heaven' and passes through each horizontal plane at its centre, that is, at the point where the equilibrium which that manifestation implies is achieved'; René Guénon, *Symbolism of the Cross*, *op.cit.*, p. 99.
40. *Ibid.*, p. 104. Cf. also the following quotations from the Hindu tradition according to A.K. Coomaraswamy, *Symbolism of the Dome*, *op.cit.*, p. 7 n.: 'The procession of the threefold spear perpetually coincides with that of these worlds' (*Jaiminiya Brahmana*, I.247); the Sun is said to 'string these worlds to Himself by the thread of the Gale of Spirit' (*Shatapatha Brahmana*, VI.7.1.17); and 'All that is here is strung on me (*Ishwara*) as rows of gems on a string'; 'I am the self seated in the hearts of all creatures' (Bhagavad Gita, VII. 7 and X.20. S. Radhakrishnan's translation, George Allen & Unwin Ltd., London, 1948).
41. *Shatapatha Brahmana*, VI.7.1.17, according to A.K. Coomaraswamy, Symbolism of the Dome, *op.cit.*, p. 7 n.
42. In another sense, this 'ground' can also be thought of as the multiple states of the being in a context which for simplicity's sake we left unmentioned.

43. Strictly speaking, the periphery consists neither of concentric squares, nor of concentric circles, but of a spiral whose successive revolutions are separated by an indefinitely small distance. We have bypassed these and other rigorous geometrical configurations (see René Guénon, *Symbolism of the Cross*, pp. 83-110) which lead to highly complex metaphysical considerations. Their relation to our theme is only limited, but we may remark that the circumambulatory process moves, in fact, along the involutions of the spiral.
44. We have remarked earlier about 'the shifts' of certain architectural elements explicitly prescribed in the *Tantrasamuccaya.* In addition to what was said before 'the shift' could well imply that metaphysical truth is never as clear-cut as the geometry of its symbol may be. There is also a protective tendency discernible in the avoidance of axial coincidence. The gates in front of the *Linga* are so disposed that the symbol could not be observed from outside the main shrine. As a note of interest we may add that the point from which the Hindu devotee would observe the *Linga* coincides with the intersection of the main axes of the whole temple. Without stretching this point too far, one may observe that the devotee himself may be identified with the vertical axis, the *Linga* 'resting in his heart'.
45. A.K. Coomaraswamy, Symbolism of the Dome, *op.cit.*, p. 9.
46. *Ibid.*, p. 7 n. Cf. *Shatapatha Brahmana* I.9.3.
47. *Ibid.*, p. 9. Cf. Mahidhara's commentary on the *Shatapatha Brahmana.*
48. *Lingobhava Skanda Purana*, according to A.K. Coomaraswamy and M.E. Noble, *Myth of the Hindus and Buddhists*, London, 1913.

GLOSSARY

Abhasa	: reflection, modality
Acarya	: spiritual father, *see* also Guru
Adharashila	: foundation stone
Adhisthana	: basement, socle
Agama	: text, treatise or scripture of traditional (derived) authority
Agni	: fire, the name of the god of fire in Vedic times; the prototype *in divinis* of the sacerdotal function
Airavata	: the name of the mythological first divine elephant
Akasha	: ether, firmament; immanent space
Alpagriha	: lit. 'small chamber', i.e. a temple of the smaller type
Amrita	: the drink of immortality extracted by the gods and demons by churning the Milky Ocean
Ananda	: beatitude, bliss, esp. divine bliss
Ananta	: 'endless'; the name of Vishnu's serpent
Angula	: measure of length, see Hasta – 24 angulas; one angula is approximately the width of the thumb, i.e. 5/6 of an inch
Ap	: water
Apara-	: non-supreme
Asura, Asuric	: demon, demonic
Atma	: self, Self, Universal Man, Brahma
Avatar	: Divine incarnation
Bhitti	: wall
Bhu	: to be, to become; 'the Earth'
Bhumi	: plane, level, tier
Bhuta	: sensible element, elementary substance, existence
Bhuta-Ganas	: Shiva's host of demons
Bija	: point, 'point-source' of the sensible order
Bindu	: point, 'point-source' of the causal order
Brahma(n)	: the Supreme Identity (absolutely unqualified)
Brahma	: the name of the Creative Principle; the personified God of creation; the Creator

Brahmana	:	officiating priest of the Brahmin caste; the second section of the Vedas
Brahmin	:	the priestly caste; member of the priestly caste; officiating priest
Bringhi	:	name of a servant of Shiva
Buddha	:	the name of the ninth incarnation of Vishnu; widely revered sage and spiritual reformer
Buddhi	:	the 'higher intellect', Logos (supra-individual faculty); also the name of Ganesha's consort
Chakra	:	wheel, node
Chit	:	consciousness, esp. divine Consciousness
Darshana	:	view, point of view; seeing; the contemplative act of seeing
Deva	:	god, angelic being
Devi	:	goddess
Dig-Gajas	:	the elephants of (the eight directions of) space
Durga	:	see Parvati
Dvara	:	door, gate
Dvarapalaka	:	gatekeeper
Dvarashakha	:	door jamb
Ekadanta	:	see Ganesha
Gajanana	:	see Ganesha
Gala	:	neck
Ganapati	:	see Ganesha
Ganesha	:	the name of Shiva's and Parvati's son; the principle of obstacles and wisdom; as a personal God, the symbol of Shiva and Ishwara; other names: Vighneshvara, Ganapati, Gajanana, Ekadanta, Vinayaka, Heramba, Lambodara, Surpakarna, Guhagraja
Garbha	:	germ, seed
Garbhagriha	:	the 'womb of the seed'; the inner chamber of the Vimana
Garbhapatra	:	the 'casket of the seed'
Garbhavinyasa	:	the ceremony of installing the 'germ of the temple' in the foundations
Ghanadvara	:	false door
Ghata	:	second part of the pillar
Gopura(m)	:	temple-gatetower
Griha	:	womb, inner chamber, esp. the inner space of the Vimana
Griva	:	neck
Guru	:	spiritual preceptor, teacher
Harmya Prasada	:	the 'high temple'

Hasta	:	measure of length, i.e. hasta = cubit = 2 padas = 24 angulas; the distance from the elbow to the tip of the middle finger
Indra	:	the name of the king of the gods in Vedic times; the prototype *in divinis* of the kingly function
Isha, Ishana	:	name of Shiva; also denoting the north-east quarter on a temple site
Ishwara	:	the name of the unmanifested Principle of Being; the first qualification of Brahma; the immanent and personal God
Jalandhara	:	name of a titan king
Jaya	:	name of a companion of Parvati
Jivatma	:	the 'living soul', the individual soul
Kalasha	:	vase, 'high vase'; the sacred pot on the top of the temple
Kali	:	see Parvati
Kaliya	:	name of the Serpent King overcome by Krishna
Kalpa	:	the cycle of time comprising 1,000 Mahayugas or 14 Manvantara-s; a single 'day' of Brahma
Kirttimukha	:	the terrifying and devouring 'Face of Glory'
Krishna	:	the name of the eighth incarnation of Vishnu; widely revered god
Kudmala	:	bud
Kumbha	:	pot, vessel, vase
Lakshmi	:	the name of Vishnu's consort; goddess of wealth
Lila	:	play, unmotivated manifestation
Linga(m)	:	ideal image, i.e. supreme symbol of Shiva; the original fiery pillar represented usually as a stone pillar placed upon its inevitable counterpart and base: the Yoni
Ma-	:	to measure; mother
Mahayuga	:	the complete cycle of four Yugas; 43,20,000 years
Makara	:	sea-monster (derived mostly from the crocodile as prototype)
Mana	:	measure
Mandala	:	closed polygon, figure, diagram
Mandapa(m)	:	pillared hall
Mandi	:	third part of the pillar
Mantra	:	incantation, enchantment, e.g. verses; the first section of the Vedas
Manvantara	:	one fourteenth part of a Kalpa; a cycle of time ending with a partial dissolution of the universe
Marma	:	vulnerable spot
Marmavedha	:	piercing of vulnerable spots
Matra	:	measure, dimension, principle; letter as definition

Maya	:	creative power, mother, divine energy, ground of manifestation, appearance, magic
Minakshi	:	the name of the 'Fish-eyed Goddess', *see* also Parvati
Moksha	:	deliverance, release
Mula	:	roof
Murugan	:	the name of Shiva's and Parvati's second son; the principle of fighting and justice; other names: Skanda, Guha, Sanmukha, Subramanya, Karttikeya
Nada	:	point, 'point-source' of the ideal order
Nadi	:	vessel, artery, esp. 'the luminous arteries of the subtle form'
Naga	:	serpent
Nala	:	stalk, lotus stalk
Nama	:	name, idea, form
Nandi	:	bull, esp. Shiva's bull, his vehicle
Narada	:	name of a legendary sage, the messenger of gods
Narayana	:	name of Vishnu as Supreme Lord
Nateshwar	:	the Lord of the Dance, i.e. Shiva
Nidhikalasha	:	the 'low vase'; the sacred pot installed in the foundation of the temple
Nirguna	:	unqualified
Om	:	(pronounced Aum) the sacred monosyllable as the symbol of Atma and Brahma
Oma	:	base (first part) of the pillar
Omkara	:	Om in its total aspect
Pada	:	leg
Padma	:	lotus
Para-	:	supreme
Parvati	:	the name of Shiva's consort; Goddess; the symbol of Maya; the symbol of Universal Substantiality; other names: Durga; Kali, Chandi, Chamunda, Uma, Sati, Minakshi
Potika	:	capital (top part) of the pillar
Pottamarai Kulam	:	the Tank of the Golden Lilies
Prajapati	:	the Lord of produced beings; the universal constructive principle; Ishwara
Prajna	:	the principal or ruler of the deep sleep, i.e. the thoughtless state in man and of formless manifestation generally; also identified with Ishwara
Prakara(m)	:	enclosure
Prakriti	:	'nature', natura naturans, substance, possibility, Universal Substantiality
Prasada	:	lit. 'settling down'; a seat, dwelling; the seat of God; temple; building, palace
Prastara	:	entablature

Prati : top moulding of the base of the temple
Pratika : traditional symbolism
Prithivi : earth, earthly substance
Puja : ritual offering to the gods performed by the Brahmins on behalf of the worshipper
Purana : collection of texts of traditional myths
Purusha : 'Person', personality, esp. Divine Personality; Essence, Essentiality; in its highest aspect Divine Impersonality

Rahu : name of the councillor of the demons; one who causes the eclipse of the moon
Rasa : flavour, essence (in liquids), savour
Ribhu : fashioner, artist
Rishi : sage, seer
Rudra : see Shiva
Rupa : shape, semblance, image, likeness, aspect

Sachchidananda : 'Being-Consciousness-Bliss', the divine qualities of Ishwara
Sadas : sacrificial shed
Saguna : qualified
Samsara : the endless cycles of manifestation; the world of appearances; the bonds of endless manifestation
Saraswati : the name of Brahma's consort; goddess
Sat, Sattva : being, unified Being in non-separate mode
Shakti : power, genius, energy (considered substantial or feminine in nature); the feminine consort of the masculine gods; the Goddess
Shastra : text, treatise or scripture of traditional (derived) authority
Shesa : 'remainder'; the name of the Serpent
Shikhara : head, dome, top part of the temple
Shilpa : art, the practice of art
Shilpin : artist
Shiva : the 'Propitious'; the name of the Transforming Principle; as a personal God the symbol of Ishwara; in its highest aspect the symbol of Brahma; other names: Isha, Rudra, Kala, Nataraja, Nateshwar, Pashupati, Sundareswar etc.
Shri Minakshi Sundareswar : the name of the Great Temple at Madura (South India) dedicated to Shiva and Parvati
Shruti : heard, audition, 'revelation', immediate authority, scripture; the Vedas
Siddhi : Ganesha's consort
Skanda : *see* Murugan
Skandha : shoulder course
Smriti : remembered, tradition, derived authority; texts of derived authority; Shastra, Sutra, Agama, Tantra, Purana

Soma	:	the moon, the Lord of germs, the divinity presiding over formation
Somanatha	:	the name of the place where an important sacred shrine was dedicated to Shiva
Stambha, Skambha	:	pillar, post, sacrificial post, 'stauros'
Sthapati	:	architect
Stupika	:	top knot, finial
Subrahmanya	:	see Murugan
Sundareswar	:	see Shiva; aspect of Shiva enshrined at Madura
Surya	:	the Sun
Sutra	:	text, treatise or scripture of traditional (derived) authority
Sutragrahi(n)	:	surveyor-draftsman
Swar, Swarga	:	the 'Sky'
Taijasa	:	the principal or ruler of the 'dream state' in man and of subtle manifestation generally
Taksaka	:	sculptor-carpenter
Tantra	:	text, treatise or scripture of traditional (derived) authority
Tantrasamuccaya	:	the name of a treatise on the science of architecture
Tantrik (c)	:	one following the spirit of the scriptures
Tapas	:	heat, fervour, disciplines generating heat (physical or otherwise); concentration
Tejas	:	fire, fiery substance
Teppa Kulam	:	the water-tank in the temple
Torana	:	gate, esp. the arch over the gate
Tribhuvana	:	the three orders of manifestation
Triloka	:	three worlds, e.g. three orders of manifestation; *see* also Tribhuvana
Trimurti	:	the threefold aspect of Ishwara
Tvastri	:	name of a titan ruler
Uma	:	*see* Parvati
Upanishad	:	'the approach to the utter destruction of ignorance' (by Shankaracharya); the last section of the Vedas
Uttara Vedi	:	the 'high altar'
Vaishwanara	:	the principle or ruler of the 'waking state' in man and of gross manifestation generally
Vajra	:	thunderbolt
Varaha	:	boar, esp. Vishnu's incarnation as a boar
Vardhaki(n)	:	builder-painter
Varuna	:	the ruler of the 'Waters'
Vastopati	:	*see* Vastupurusha
Vastu	:	existence
Vastu	:	dwelling place, planned site

Vastudeva, Vastu-Naga : *see* Vastupurusha

Vastu-Puja : the ritual offering to the deity presiding over the building of the temple

Vastupurusha : 'indwelling personality', Divine Immanence; other names: Vastudeva, Vastu-Naga, Vastopati

Vastupurusha-Mandala : the sacred diagram or the geometrical image of the residing Divine Personality

Vastu-Shastra : traditional text dealing with the science of architecture as sacred art

Vayu : wind; name of the Vedic god of wind; air; breath

Veda(-s) (Vedic) : the sacred scriptures of the orthodox Hindu tradition in four parts (Rig-,Yajur-, Sama-, Atharva-); first authority, Shruti

Vedanta : end of the Veda

Vedha : piercing

Vedi : altar, sacrificial altar

Venu : central shaft of the Vimana

Vighneswara : see Ganesha

Vijaya : name of a companion of Parvati

Vimana : lit. 'possessing varied measures'; temple, esp. the essential core of a temple-town

Vinayaka : *see* Ganesha

Virakanda : fourth part of the pillar

Vishnu : the name of the Maintaining Principle; as a personal God the symbol of Ishwara; in its highest aspect the symbol of Brahma; *see* also Narayana

Vishvakarma : the name of the divine prototype of the architectural function

Vithika : interspace

Yajamana : sacrificer, patron of building

Yajna : sacrifice

Yali : fiery monster, beast

Yama : the name of the Vedic god of death

Yanman : plinth

Yoga : union, yoking; sill in action

Yantra : 'device', sacred diagram, geometrical representation of a deity

Yoganala : lit. the 'vessel of yoking'; funnel-shaped tube built into the foundation of the temple

Yoni : source, matrix, measure, primordial route; the square pedestal under the Linga; the inevitable substantial element in the Linga-Yoni combination as the supreme symbol of Shiva

Yuga : a cycle of time, a 'world age', the four Yugas: Krita (perfect), Treta (triad), Dvapara (duad) and Kali (worst) in the proportion of 4:3:2:1 make up one Mahayuga

SOURCES AND BIBLIOGRAPHY

1. TRADITIONAL TEXTS

Shruti

Atharva Veda, Bombay, 1895-98 (W.D. Whitney, Harvard Oriental Series)
Brihadaranyaka Upanishad, Poona, 1915
Chhandogya Upanishad, Poona, 1915 (Ganganath Jha, Poona, 1942)
Jaiminiya Upanishad Brahmana, Lahore, 1921
Mandukya Upanishad, Poona, 1915
Rig Veda, Bombay, 1889-90 (H.H. Wilson, London)
Shatapatha Brahmana, Bombay, 1942 (J. Eggeling, *The Sacred Books of the East*)
Taittiriya Samhita, Mysore Gov. Oriental Series, 1894-98 (A.B. Keith, Harvard Oriental Series)
Taittiriya Brahmana, Poona, 1898

Translation and Commentary :

Nikhilananda, Swami, *The Upanishads*, Phoenix House Ltd., London, 1957

Smriti

Bhagavad Gita, Bombay, 1909 (Radhakrishnan, London)
Brahma Sutras, Bombay, 1919
Brihat Samhita, Vizianagvam Series, 1895-97 (H. Kern)
Mahanirvana Tantra, Calcutta, 1919 (A. Avalon, Calcutta)
Manasara, Benares (P.K. Acharya, Oxford University Press, 1932)
Manu Smriti, Bombay
Matangalila, Bombay
Samarangana Sutradhara, Baroda, 1924-25
Shilparatna, Trivandrum, 1922
Shiva Purana, Calcutta, 1885
Skanda Purana, Bombay, 1910
Vedanta Sutra, Bombay, 1919

Vishnu Purana, Bombay, 1921
Tantraraja Tantra, Calcutta, 1919
Tantrasamuccaya, Trivandrum, 1919-21 (N.V. Mallaya, Annamalainagar)

Translation and Commentary :

Radhakrishnan, S., *The Bhagavad Gita*, George Allen and Unwin Ltd., London, 1956
N.V. Mallaya, *Studies in Sanscrit Texts on Temple Architecture (with special refereces to Tantrassmuccaya)*, Annamalai University Publications, Annamalainagar, 1949

2. RECENT WORKS ON DOCTRINE, SYMBOLISM AND ART

René Guénon :

Les États multiples de l'être, Les Éditions Véga, Paris, 1932
East and West, Luzac, London, 1941
Introduction to the Study of the Hindu Doctrine, Luzac, London, 1945
Man and His Becoming according to the Vedanta, Luzac, London, 1945
La Grande Triade, Revue de la Table Ronde, Nancy, 1946
The Reign of Quantity and its Signs in the Times, Luzac, London, 1953
The Symbolism of the Cross, Luzac, London, 1958

Ananda K. Coomaraswamy :

Myths of the Hindus and Buddhists (with M.E. Noble), London, 1913
The Dancing Shiva, Sunwise Turn, New York, 1918
History of Indian and Indonesian Art, Goldston, London, 1927
Yaksas, Part II, Smithonian Institution, Washington, 1931
Elements of Buddhist Iconography, Harvard University Press, Cambridge, Mass., 1935
'Symbolism of the Dome', *The Indian Historical Quarterly*, Vol. XIV, No. 1, March 1938
Time and Eternity, *Artibus Asiae*, Ascona (Switzerland), 1947
The Transformation of Nature in Art, Dover, New York, 1956
Hinduism and Buddhism, Philosophical Library, New York

Stella Kramrisch :

The Hindu Temple, 2 Vols., University of Calcutta, 1946

Titus Burckhardt :

The Genesis of the Hindu Temple, *Études Traditionelles*, Oct.-Nov., 1953 (A.B. Snodgrass' unpublished translation)
Principes et Méthodes de l'Art sacré (Derain, Lyons, 1958)

Frithjof Schuon :

L'Oeil du Coeur, Gallimard, Bagneux (Seine), 1950
The Transcendent Unity of Religions, Faber and Faber, London, 1953
Spiritual Perspectives and Human Facts, Faber and Faber, London, 1956

Heinrich Zimmer :

Myths and Symbols in Indian Art and Civilization, Bollingen Series, VI, Pantheon Books Inc., New York, 1946

F.D.K. Bosh :

The Golden Germ (An Introduction to Indian Symbolism), Mouton & Co., The Hague (Netherlands), 1960

I.A. Gopinatha Rao :

Elements of Hindu Iconography, Madras, 1914-16

3. DESCRIPTIVE AND PICTORIAL WORKS

Behera, K.S., *Konarak: The Heritage of Mankind*, 2 vols., Aryan Books International, New Delhi, 1996
Bhattacharya, *Study of Vastuvidya or Cannons of Indian Architecture*, Varanasi, 1963
Bonner, A. and Sadasiva Rath Sarma, *New Light on the Sun Temple of Konarak*, Varanasi, Chowkhamba, 1972
Bussagli, M., *Oriental Architecture*, Heinemann, New York, 1973
Case, Margaret H., *Govindadeva: A Dialogue in Stone*, New Delhi, 1996
Deva, Krishna, *Temples of India*, 2 vols., Aryan Books International, New Delhi, 1995
Fergusson, James, *History of Indian and Eastern Architecture*, R.P. Spiers, London, 1891
Frédéric, Luis, *Indian Temples and Sculpture*, Thames & Hudson, London, 1959
Goetz, H., *India, Art of World Series*, Methuen, London, 1959
Guenon, R., *Symboles fondamentauz de la Science Sacree*, Gallimard, Paris, 1962
India: Photographs and Drawings from the Office of Curator of Monuments, 1896
Murray-Lothian, *Handbook for Travellers in India, Pakistan, Burma, and Ceylon*, 17th ed., London, 1955
Nowrath, E.A., *Indien und China, Meisterwerke der Baukunst und Plastik*, Wien, 1938
Odette Monod-Bruhl, *Indian Temples*, 2nd ed., Oxford University Press, London, 1952
Pichard, Pierre, *Tanjavur Brhadisvara: An Architectural Study*, New Delhi, 1995
Rowland, Benjamin, *The Architecture and Art of India, Buddhist, Hindu, Jain*, Penguin Books, London, 1953
Volwahsen, A., *Living Architecture, Indian*, Macdonald, London, 1969

INDEX